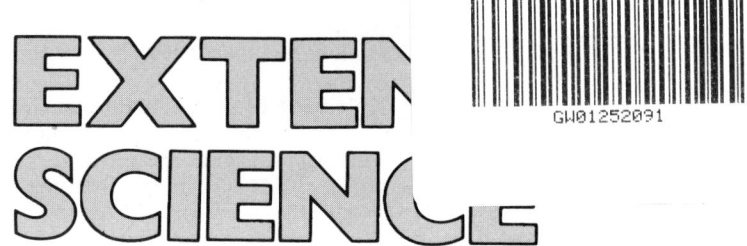

AIR

Selected Topics

Second Edition

E N Ramsden BSc PhD DPhil
R E Lee BSc

Stanley Thornes (Publishers) Ltd

© E N Ramsden and R E Lee 1983, 1990

All rights reserved. No part* of this publication may be reproduced or transmitted in any form or by any means, electronic or mechanical, including photocopy, recording, or any information storage and retrieval system, without permission in writing from the publisher or under licence from the Copyright Licensing Agency Limited. Further details of such licences (for reprographic reproduction) may be obtained from the Copyright Licensing Agency Limited, of 33-4 Alfred Place, London WC1E 7DP.

First published in 1983 by
Stanley Thornes (Publishers) Ltd
Old Station Drive
Leckhampton
CHELTENHAM GL53 0DN

Reprinted 1986
Reprinted 1987
Second edition 1990

*An exception is made for the word puzzles on pp. 7, 15, 25, 62 and 70. Teachers may photocopy a puzzle to save time for a pupil who would otherwise need to copy from his/her copy of the book. Teachers wishing to make multiple copies of a word puzzle for distribution to a class without individual copies of the book must apply to the publishers in the normal way.

British Library Cataloguing in Publication Data

Ramsden, E. N.
   Air.
   1. Air
   I. Title   II. Lee, R. E.   III. Series
   551.51

ISBN 0-7487-0449-3

Typeset by Tech-Set, Gateshead, Tyne & Wear.
Printed and bound in Great Britain by Ebenezer Baylis & Son, Worcester.

CONTENTS

Chapter 1   **We Need Air**

What is air?	1
Oxygen	1
Who needs pure oxygen?	2
Questions on oxygen	5
Crossword on oxygen	7
The importance of nitrogen	8
Questions on nitrogen	13
Crossword on nitrogen	15
The importance of carbon dioxide	16
The greenhouse effect	17
Saving the rain forest	19
Questions on the greenhouse effect	21
More about photosynthesis and respiration	22
Questions on carbon dioxide	24
Crossword on carbon dioxide	25
The noble gases	26
Some experiments on air	27
(1) Some experiments on photosynthesis	27
(2) Measure your lung power	28
(3) What volume of air passes through your lungs in 24 hours?	28
(4) Does the air you breathe out contain more carbon dioxide than ordinary air?	29
(5) How do clouds form?	29

Chapter 2   **Pollutants**

What are pollutants?	30
Smog: the silent killer	31
Photochemical smog	33
Temperature inversion: Los Angeles	34
Sulphur dioxide strikes again: The Acropolis	34
Acid rain	37
Questions on sulphur and acid rain	42
Aerosols and the ozone layer: push-button convenience or push-button cancer?	44
Saving the ozone layer	47
Questions on the ozone layer	48
Lead in petrol: professors knock anti-knock	49
Questions on petrol	51
Carbon monoxide: the invisible killer	52
Questions on engines	54
Mercury: the Mad Hatter's complaint	54
Fluorides	55
Questions for discussion	55
Cigarette smoke	55
Questions and activities on smoking	57
Questions for discussion	61
Wordfinder on pollution	62
Radioactivity	63
Nuclear power stations	63
Nuclear accidents	63
Testing of nuclear weapons	65
Storage of radioactive waste	66
Some pollution activities	67
(1) How pure is the air you breathe? The lichens will tell you	67
(2) Collecting dust	67
(3) Looking at smoke	68
(4) What gases are put into the air when coal burns?	68
(5) What gases are put into the air when petroleum products burn?	68
(6) Making and testing sulphur dioxide	68
(7) Does sulphur dioxide affect plants?	68
(8) What do cigarettes deposit in your lungs?	69
Questions on pollution	69
Crossword on air pollution	70
Summary of pollution	71
What can be done?	71
More questions on pollution	72

Answer to wordfinder on p. 62	73	Index	74
Answers to numerical questions	73		

PREFACE

We wrote the first edition of this book because the subject of air and the pollution of air interests us. We hoped that children would find the topics which we selected interesting and come to realise the importance of conserving our environment.

The first edition of the book was used as extension material in junior chemistry courses, as part of general science courses and as background material for older pupils following certificate courses. When GCSE was introduced, teachers found that the book, in common with other titles in the Extending Science series, was a source of the new-style material in the GCSE syllabuses.

The Extending Science series began as a set of books dealing with the social, economic, environmental and technological aspects of science. Since the series began, these aspects of science have been incorporated into the National Criteria for GCSE and into the National Curriculum. Now that these social aspects of science are part of mainstream curriculum science, the Extending Science books are being used in GCSE modular science courses.

In the second edition of *Air*, we have brought topics up to date and also included more opportunities for pupils to practise their skills in interpreting and analysing data and in devising experiments of their own. The book is not intended to provide the complete coverage of air that is required for examination courses: information and experiments that can be found readily in textbooks have been omitted.

E N Ramsden
Beverley, Humberside, 1990

R E Lee
St George's College, Weybridge, 1990

ACKNOWLEDGEMENTS

We are grateful to Mr J R Dennison and Mr B Rogers, who read the original draft and made many helpful suggestions. Miss Laura Hale has given invaluable assistance with the diagrams, and Mr D F Manley has made significant improvements in the crosswords and supplied the wordfinder. We thank our publishers for the enthusiasm and attention to detail which have gone into the production of this book, and our families for their encouragement.

The authors and publishers are grateful to the following who provided photographs and gave permission for reproduction:

All-Sport Photographic Ltd (cover); The Associated Press Ltd (p. 65); British Aerospace Corporation (p. 46); The British Interplanetary Society Ltd (p. 5); The British Oxygen Co Ltd (pp. 3, 4); British Steel Corporation (p. 6); J. Allan Cash Ltd (p. 40); Peter Crawshaw (p. 26); Greek Tourist Agency (pp. 35, 36); Imperial Chemical Industries Ltd (pp. 11, 12, 13); Mansell Collection (p. 53); National Vegetable Research Station (p. 8); Planet Earth Pictures (main cover, pp. 2, 27); Popperfoto (p. 32); Whitbread & Company PLC (p. 50).

CHAPTER 1

WE NEED AIR

WHAT IS AIR?

Air is a mixture of gases. Oxygen and nitrogen are the main components. Roughly one-fifth of the air is oxygen and four-fifths is nitrogen. Other gases are present too. The noble gases (helium, neon, argon, krypton and xenon) form 1 per cent of the air. Carbon dioxide forms 0.03 per cent. Water vapour is present in variable amounts—a tropical forest will have more water vapour in the air around it than a desert. Pollutants are also present. The diagram below shows the composition of air in percentages by volume.

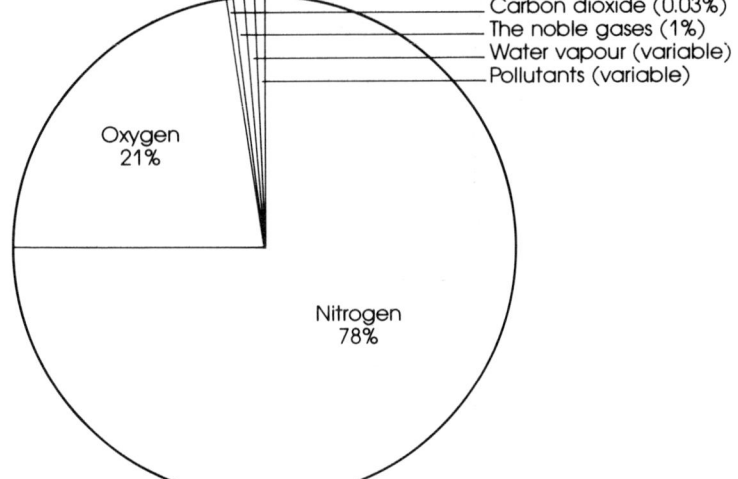

Approximate composition of air by volume

The amount of pollution depends on whether the air is fresh, country air or whether it is city air, full of factory smoke and car exhaust fumes. Factories send smoke and grit into the air. Car exhausts expel sulphur dioxide and carbon monoxide into the air.

OXYGEN

A fifth of the air is oxygen. From our point of view, the most important chemical reaction in which oxygen takes part is respiration. If we breathed pure oxygen, all our body

1

processes would go on much faster than they do, and we would soon wear ourselves out. The nitrogen in the air dilutes the oxygen and brings it down to a level suitable for us to breathe.

For some purposes, pure oxygen is needed. It is obtained from air.

Who needs pure oxygen?

Mountaineers need extra oxygen. They find that as they climb higher and higher up a mountain the air becomes thinner and thinner. They start gasping in great mouthfuls of air, but it still does not give them the oxygen they need. They find they have less and less energy as they go higher and higher. If they carry oxygen cylinders on their backs, they can give themselves a gentle stream of oxygen. This gives them the energy they need to keep going.

Pilots flying at high altitudes have the same problem. At a distance of 3 miles from the ground, the air pressure is only

Deep-sea diver using oxygen mixture

half that at ground level. Pilots flying unpressurised aircraft carry oxygen cylinders and breathing masks for high flying.

Divers take oxygen cylinders with them for working under water. A diver like Jacques Cousteau wears a mask connected to a cylinder of oxygen mixed with helium on his back when he goes exploring under water.

Many victims of car and motorcycle accidents need oxygen even if they do not have chest injuries. A blow to the back of the head can affect the part of the brain which controls breathing. Then the brain will stop telling the lungs to do their job. The victim is rushed to hospital and connected to a breathing machine (a respirator). The machine pumps oxygen into the victim's lungs. After a time, the brain recovers from the blow it has received and takes over again. It takes charge of the lungs, and the patient can breathe normally again.

Other accident victims need oxygen too. People rescued from smoke-filled rooms and people rescued from drowning need oxygen. If their lungs are full of smoke or water, they cannot be filled with air. Working at only a part of their normal

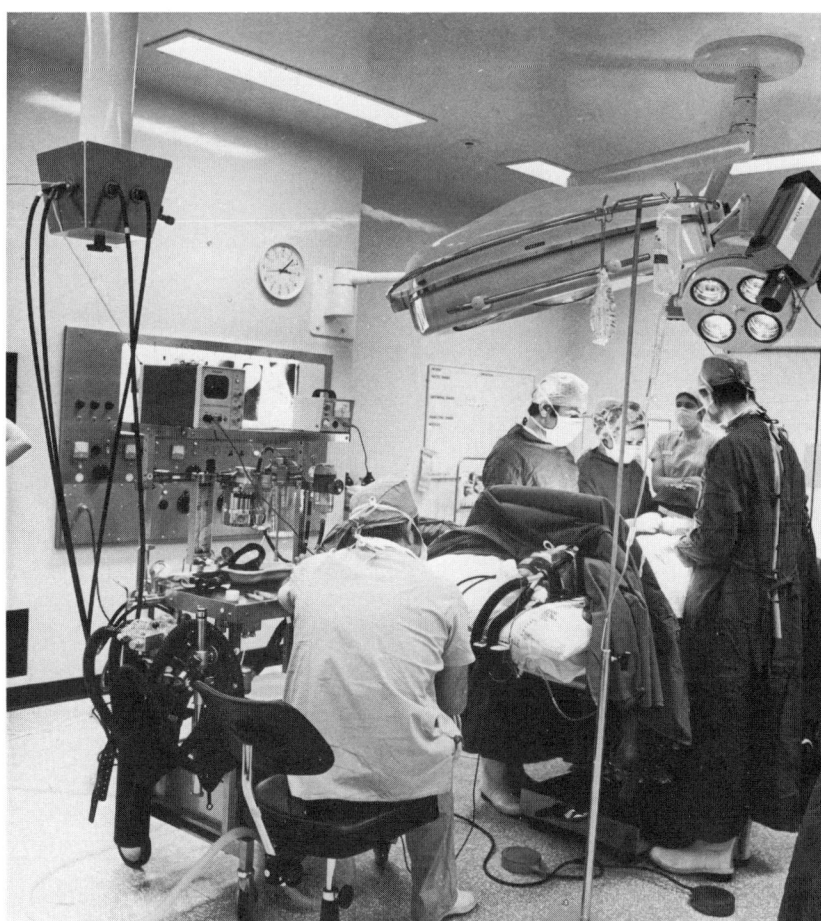

Oxygen in the operating theatre

capacity, they need pure oxygen, instead of air. Asthmatics and pneumonia patients also need oxygen as their lungs contain fluid. A patient who is having an operation is given anaesthetic mixed with oxygen.

Oxygen is used in industry. Things burn much more fiercely in oxygen than in air, with a hotter flame. A very hot flame is needed for jobs such as cutting metal and welding metal. Such a flame can be obtained by burning a fuel in oxygen. The oxyacetylene torch burns the gas acetylene (or ethyne as it is now called) in oxygen. A temperature of 3000°C is obtained. The photograph below shows metalworkers using a thermic lance on the Longships lighthouse.

The steel industry uses an enormous amount of oxygen. A tonne of oxygen is needed for every tonne of steel produced. Steel works have their own oxygen plants on the same site.

Thermic lance

When iron is made into steel, it is melted and then a jet of oxygen is directed on to the surface of the molten metal. The carbon which it contains burns to form the gas carbon monoxide.

All space flights need oxygen. Space craft carry fuel, and they also carry oxygen for the fuel to burn in. The Saturn rockets which were used to lift American astronauts into orbit for their journey to the Moon carried over 2200 tonnes of liquid oxygen. The first stage, while the jets were roaring, burned 450 tonnes of kerosene in 1800 tonnes of oxygen. Stages two and three were powered by hydrogen burning in oxygen. There was also oxygen for the astronauts to breathe.

The US Space Shuttle: the top of the large external tank is full of liquid oxygen for launch; it is filled through the large slab-type structures partly covering the Shuttle's wings

QUESTIONS ON OXYGEN

1 What fraction of the air (by volume) is oxygen?

2 Is it better for you to breathe air or pure oxygen?

3 Name three kinds of patient who might be given pure oxygen in hospital.

4 Name three kinds of explorer who would need to take oxygen with them.

Steel-making

5 State three uses which are made of pure oxygen in industry.

6 Name two processes which use up oxygen and one process which gives oxygen to the air. Is there any danger that we might run out of oxygen?

7 Draw a wall poster showing one of the explorers you have mentioned in Question (4).

8 Describe one way in which pure oxygen is used to fight pollution of (a) air, and (b) water.

CROSSWORD ON OXYGEN

First, trace this grid on to a piece of paper (or photocopy this page). Then fill in the answers. Do not write on this page.

Across

1. This place needs oxygen for sick people (8)
6. See 12 across
10. See 5 down
11. You cannot breathe if your lungs are full of this (5)
12, 6. This fraction of 24 across is oxygen (3-5)
13. Short for postscript (2)
16. This kind of flame is very hot (12)
18. The 24 across on a mountain is ____ (4)
19. It may help you if you get lost (3)
20. Container for ashes (3)
21. Someone who uses petrol to travel (6)
23. See 15 down
24. A mixture of gases we breathe (3)
25. It may give you a disease (4)

Down

1. Hello! (2)
2. See 5 down
3. To make this metal you need plenty of oxygen (5)
4. A measure of acidity (2)
5, 7, 2, 10 across. Give this to someone who is not breathing (3, 4, 2, 4)
7. See 5 down
8. Someone in space who needs oxygen (9)
9. Someone climbing who needs oxygen (11)
13. Patients with this lung complaint need oxygen (9)
14. Store oxygen in this (8)
15-22, 23 across. On this person's back is a cylinder of oxygen (4-3, 5)
17. The flame of 16 across is used for ____ metals (7)
22. See 15 down

THE IMPORTANCE OF NITROGEN

To us, the important part of the air seems to be oxygen. For plants, nitrogen is a matter of life and death. Plants use nitrogen to build up plant proteins. Most plants cannot use the nitrogen in the air. Some can: these are leguminous plants (such as peas, beans and clover) in which certain kinds of bacteria thrive. These bacteria can use nitrogen from the air and build it up into proteins. They are called *nitrogen-fixing bacteria*. Most plants use nitrogen compounds, not gaseous nitrogen. Ammonium compounds and nitrates are compounds which contain nitrogen and are soluble, so that plants can absorb them from the soil through their roots.

When plants die, the nitrogen compounds return to the soil. Whenever plants are eaten by animals, the plant proteins are

Crop treated with low-nitrogen fertiliser on the right and with a high-nitrogen fertiliser on the left

transformed into animal proteins. When the animals die, these compounds return to the soil. Any excess protein which animals do not need is changed into urea, and excreted in urine. This returns it to the soil where it can be used again by plants. This natural cycle of events is called the *nitrogen cycle* and is illustrated below.

The nitrogen cycle

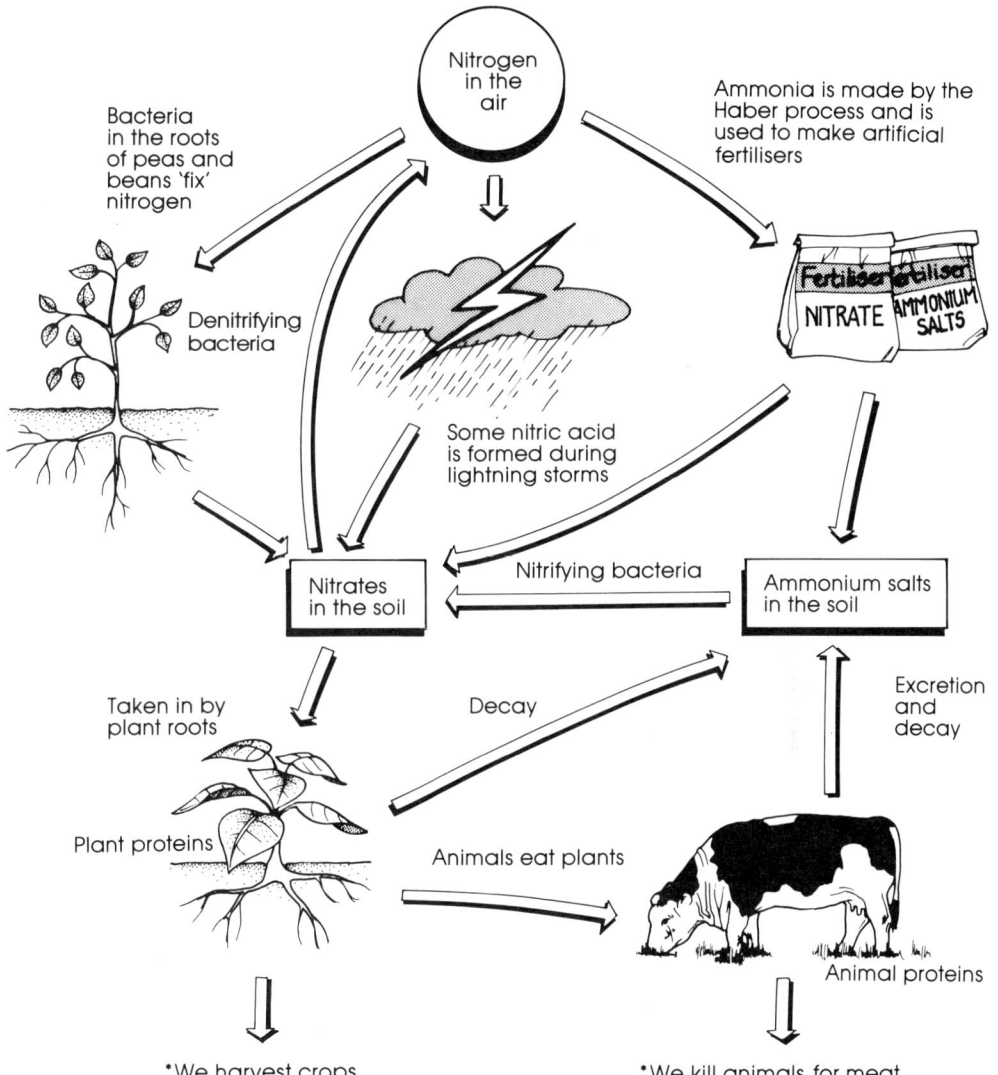

*These are two ways in which we take nitrogen out of the natural cycle. We have to add fertilisers to make up the loss.

We interfere with the natural cycle. We do not allow plants and animals to decay and return to the soil. We do not allow all our body waste to return to the soil. We send it to the sewage-works and only a part of it is used to enrich the soil. We have to put more nitrogen back into the ground, and we do this by using fertilisers. Fertilisers contain nitrogen in the form of ammonium salts or nitrates.

Ever since the beginning of the nineteenth century, farmers have needed fertiliser in addition to manure from their livestock. As the population grew, farmers needed to grow more crops to the acre. European farmers began importing *guano* from South America. Guano is a fertiliser which consists of bird droppings. Off the coast of Peru are some lonely little rocky islands inhabited only by seabirds. The birds had never been disturbed, and over the years great mounds of bird droppings had built up. They were just what the farmers of Europe needed. Shiploads of guano crossed the Atlantic from 1800 to 1900. South America was not densely populated and the people of Peru did not need extra fertiliser so they were happy to sell their guano to Europe. By 1900 the supply of guano was exhausted.

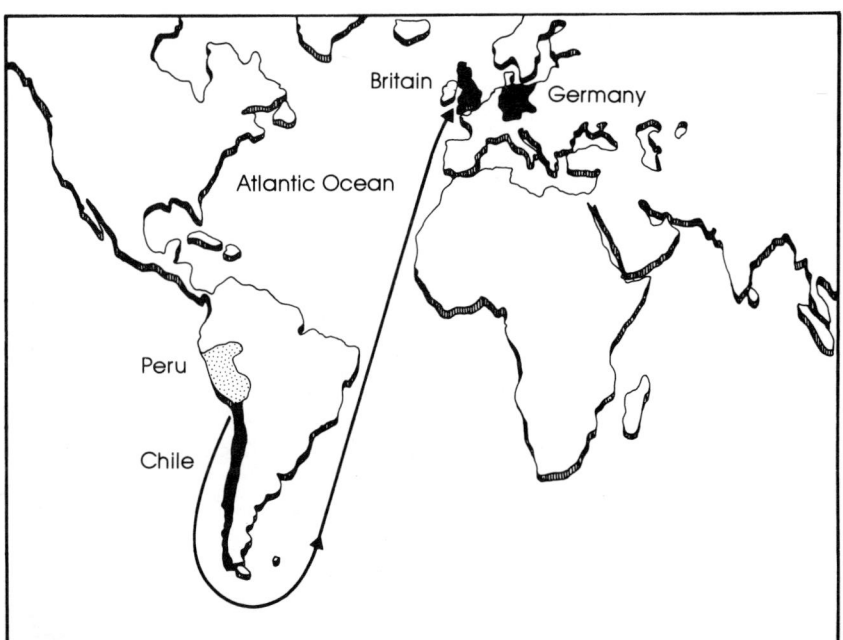

The fertiliser route

Another source of fertiliser had been discovered in South America. As the guano was running out in Peru, the supply of *Chile nitre* was increasing. Vast deposits of sodium nitrate had been discovered in Chile. People called it Chile nitre, and shipped it across to Europe by the boatload from 1850 onwards. By 1900, the deposits were not so vast as they had been 50 years earlier. Scientists in Europe began to plan for the next stage of the quest for fertilisers. Where would they turn to when the deposits of Chile nitre ran out?

There is plenty of nitrogen in the air. If only it could be turned into an ammonium compound, it could be used as a fertiliser. Chemists started working on the problem. It was not easy. In fact, it was a tough nut to crack. Nitrogen is not reactive, and it is very difficult to get it to combine with anything.

The problem was cracked by a German chemist called Fritz Haber. He found a way of making ammonia from air and water, coke and scrap iron. None of these was in short supply! Haber found that it was possible to make nitrogen combine with hydrogen to form ammonia. He heated the gases to 500°C and compressed them to 175 times atmospheric pressure. In the presence of a metal catalyst, 8 per cent of the gases reacted to form ammonia. Haber made this discovery in 1908.

Another German chemist called Carl Bosch designed an industrial plant which would make ammonia on a large scale. He found a way of making hydrogen from steam and red-hot coke. Nitrogen was obtained from the air, by fractional distillation of liquid air. Bosch discovered that iron made a good catalyst for the Haber process. He finished constructing an industrial plant for the manufacture of ammonia in 1913.

The ICI ammonia plant at Billingham

When the First World War (1914–1918) started, Germany was able to make all the fertiliser that the country needed. She still wanted Chile nitre, however, because it was the only source of nitric acid. Nitric acid was used for making ammunition and bombs which contain compounds such as nitroglycerine (used in dynamite) and trinitrotoluene (TNT). Britain used her navy to stop German ships crossing the Atlantic with cargoes of Chile nitre. The German generals were fast running out of ammunition and said they could not continue to fight a war without more supplies of nitric acid.

Haber came to the rescue again, as scientists do, by pointing out that their home-made ammonia could be oxidised to nitric acid. Another chemist called Wilhelm Ostwald worked out the details of making the reaction into an industrial process. He passed air and ammonia over a heated platinum catalyst. Oxides of nitrogen were formed and dissolved in water to give nitric acid.

A modern ammonia converter (ICI Billingham)

The German generals were delighted. Ammunition from ammonia! It goes to show that, in peace and in war, a country needs good chemists. But the generals took too large a share of the ammonia produced. While they built up their stocks of armaments, the farmers' stocks of fertilisers ran down. The harvests of 1917 and 1918 were miserable, and the Germans were short of food. This was one of the factors which led to Germany losing the war in 1918.

Haber's work on making ammonia from nitrogen and hydrogen now benefits people of all nations. In 1918, he was given a Nobel Prize for his work. In 1931, Bosch also received a Nobel Prize. A Nobel Prize is one of the highest honours a scientist can receive.

A tractor spreading nitrogenous fertiliser

QUESTIONS ON NITROGEN

Do not write on this page.

1 What fraction of the air (by volume) is nitrogen?

2 Animals obtain nitrogen compounds from eating plants. Where do plants obtain their nitrogen compounds? What kinds of nitrogen compounds do plants use? Are there any plants that can use nitrogen gas?

3 What do people mean by the 'nitrogen cycle'? Explain two ways in which we interfere with this natural cycle by removing nitrogen. What must we do to make up for this?

4 What is Nature's way of fertilising the soil?

5 Supply words for the blanks in this passage.

Farmers use nitrogen compounds to fertilise the soil. These compounds are _____ salts and _____. Both these types of compound _____ in water. They need to be _____ in water so that plants can absorb them through their roots. Plants use these compounds to make _____. Animals eat plants and convert plant _____ into animal _____.

6 Supply words for the blanks in this passage.

The first person to make ammonia from nitrogen was _____. He studied ways of making nitrogen combine with _____ to make ammonia. He found that the yield of ammonia increased if _____ pressure was used. He used a moderately high temperature. To make the yield of ammonia higher, he used a _____. The reaction was turned into an industrial process by _____. He made _____ from air and _____ from steam and red-hot coke. He used iron as the _____.

7 The table shows figures for the worldwide use of nitrogen fertilisers.

Year	Nitrogen fertilisers (thousands of tonnes)
1905	360
1925	1200
1945	2000
1965	19 000
1979	57 200
1982	61 000

(a) On graph paper, plot the mass of fertiliser against the year.
(b) Calculate the increase in the use of fertilisers between (i) 1925 and 1945 and (ii) 1945 and 1965.
(c) Give an approximate figure for the ratio
$$\frac{\text{fertiliser used in 1982}}{\text{fertiliser used in 1925}}.$$

8 A research worker at an agricultural research station made a study of two plots of land. Plot A contained grass only, and Plot B contained clover as well as grass. The scientist measured the nitrogen content of the soil over a period of 80 days. The diagram below shows the results obtained.
(a) Explain the shape of the graph for Plot A.
(b) Explain why the nitrogen content of the soil in Plot B changes (i) in the first 10 days (ii) between 10 and 40 days.

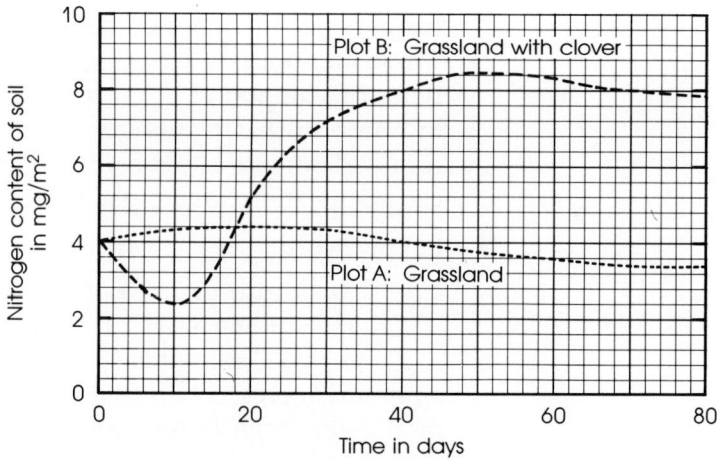

CROSSWORD ON NITROGEN

First, trace this grid on to a piece of paper (or photocopy this page). Then fill in the answers. Do not write on this page.

Across

1. He made ammonia (5)
5. Someone who buys 11 across for their fields (6)
6. A nitrogen ____ doesn't have two wheels! (5)
8. Yields go ____ when the soil is enriched (2)
11. These enrich the soil (11)
13. If the ground is ____, water can seep through (6)
14. The 5 across wants ____ skies for bringing in the 3 down (5)
15. When plants ____, nitrogen compounds return to the soil (3)
16. A cereal grown by 5 across (5)
18. He made hydrogen from steam (5)

Down

2. The way in which animals return nitrogen to the soil (9)
3. 5 across is happy with a good one (7)
4. They are grown by 5 across (5)
7. In wartime these nitrogen compounds are in demand (10)
9. In peacetime 7 down are used to ____ buildings (8)
10. Plants build up these nitrogen compounds (8)
12. Where guano came from (4)
17. A serious chest illness (2)

15

THE IMPORTANCE OF CARBON DIOXIDE

The percentage of carbon dioxide in the air is only 0.03 per cent. This may seem like next to nothing, but it is a vitally important part of the air. Plants need carbon dioxide. They use it in the process of *photosynthesis*. In this process, plants build up sugars and starches from carbon dioxide and water.

Because plants contain sugars and starches, they make nourishing food. We eat plants, and we eat animals which feed on plants. If plants ever become short of carbon dioxide, this food chain will break down, and we shall be short of food.

The percentage of carbon dioxide in the air is kept constant by a number of processes called the *carbon cycle* (see below).

The carbon cycle

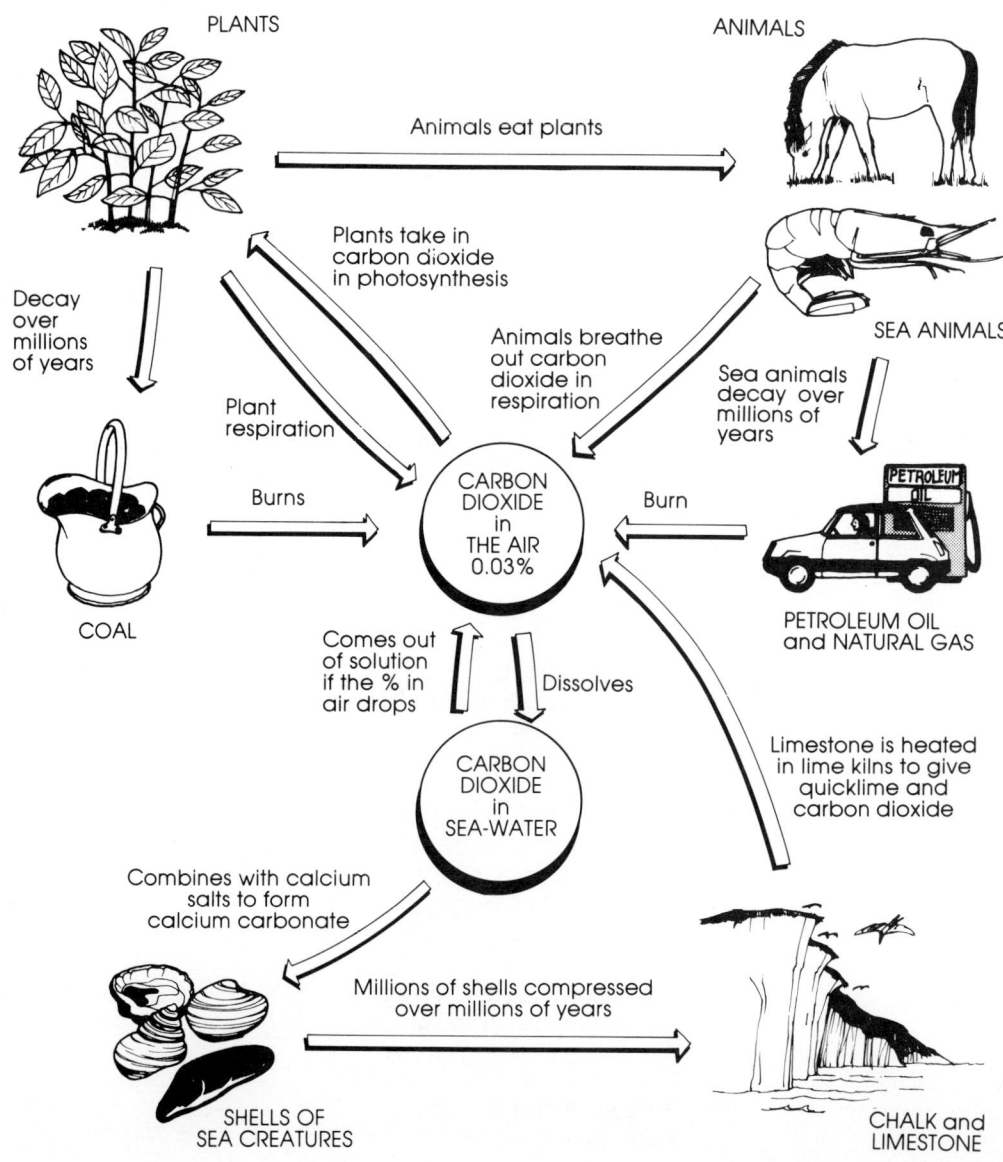

Some of these processes put carbon dioxide into the air. Burning petrol, coal and natural gas puts carbon dioxide into the air. We put carbon dioxide into the air as we breathe. Some processes take carbon dioxide out of the air. Photosynthesis is one. Carbon dioxide dissolving in the sea is another. If the level of carbon dioxide in the air rises, some carbon dioxide dissolves in the sea. If the level of carbon dioxide in the air falls, some carbon dioxide comes out of solution in the sea.

The sea contains dissolved carbon dioxide and dissolved calcium salts. Sea-living animals use calcium salts and carbon dioxide to make calcium carbonate. This is what their shells are made of. When sea creatures die, their flesh decays but their shells do not. They sink to the bottom of the sea. Over millions of years, they grow into deposits of calcium carbonate, limestone. We heat limestone in kilns to give calcium oxide, quicklime. This is used for making mortar and cement. During the heating in a lime kiln, limestone breaks down to give carbon dioxide.

Could anything upset the carbon cycle? We interfere with the natural cycle when we chop trees down. Huge areas of forest have been cut down in South America. This seems a good idea because it is dense, tropical forest which makes the area difficult to live in and impossible to cultivate. There is a danger in cutting down forests. It concerns an action of carbon dioxide called the *greenhouse effect*.

THE GREENHOUSE EFFECT

Energy from the Sun falls on the Earth and warms it up. The Earth radiates heat energy. The balance between the heat gained from the Sun and the heat lost into space keeps the Earth at a mean temperature of 15°C. The radiation which the Earth sends out is *infrared* radiation. It is absorbed by water vapour, carbon dioxide and other gases in the atmosphere (e.g. methane, oxides of nitrogen and chlorofluorocarbons, CFCs). These gases radiate some heat back towards the Earth and send some into space. They act as a blanket, keeping the Earth warm. Without this 'blanket', the Earth would be at a temperature of −20°C, and life would be impossible.

This action of carbon dioxide and the other gases has been called the *greenhouse effect*. The gases are said to act like the glass in a greenhouse. The diagram on the next page shows how the glass allows sunlight to pass through but reflects radiation from the plants back into the greenhouse.

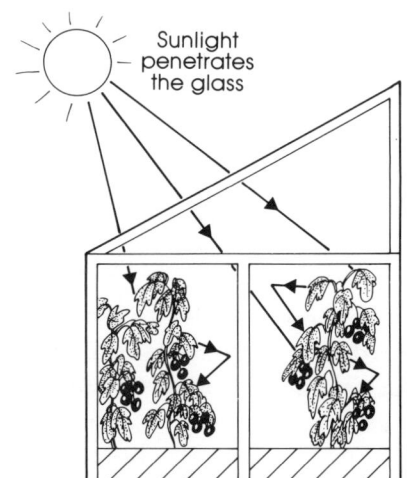

The greenhouse effect

As more and more *fossil fuels* (petrol, coal and natural gas) are burnt, more carbon dioxide and water vapour are sent into the atmosphere. The 'blanket' is becoming thicker, and as a result the Earth is warming up. Between 1880 and 1980, the surface of the Earth warmed up by 0.75°C. It is forecast that by the year 2050 the temperature will have increased by 2–3°C. Scientists predict that the Poles will warm up more than the tropics. If we do nothing about it, the Earth's temperature will continue to rise. Then there will come a time when the North and South Poles are not cold enough to keep their ice caps permanently frozen. If the temperature of the Poles were to rise above 0°C, the polar ice would start to melt and flow into the oceans. Low-lying areas of land would be covered by the sea. Holland would be flooded; East Anglia and Lincolnshire would disappear into the North Sea. Vast areas of Bangladesh and Thailand would disappear. Other countries would suffer droughts and some areas would become deserts.

Much of the carbon dioxide in the atmosphere comes from the burning of fossil fuels. As developing countries industrialise, they burn more fossil fuels to supply the energy they need. About half of the carbon dioxide formed goes into the air; the rest dissolves in the oceans. No one can say whether the oceans will be able to absorb carbon dioxide at this rate for ever. The oceans may become saturated with carbon dioxide. Then a rise in temperature would make the carbon dioxide dissolved in the sea come out of solution. The greenhouse effect of the carbon dioxide released would lead to a further rise in temperature.

What can be done to stop the build-up of carbon dioxide and other greenhouse gases? One way to cut down on the production of carbon dioxide is to stop burning petrol. We should then have to look for other sources of energy for our cars, lorries and trains. The combustion of coal and oil in power stations is another major source of carbon dioxide. Nuclear power stations do not suffer from this drawback (see Extending Science 9: *Nuclear Power*). Power stations which use wind energy, waterfalls, tides, waves and solar energy do not produce carbon dioxide (see Extending Science 7: *Energy*).

Substances called *CFCs* (chlorofluorocarbons) are used in aerosols and refrigerators. They are more powerful greenhouse gases than carbon dioxide. The steps being taken to reduce the level of CFCs in the atmosphere are discussed on pp. 47–8.

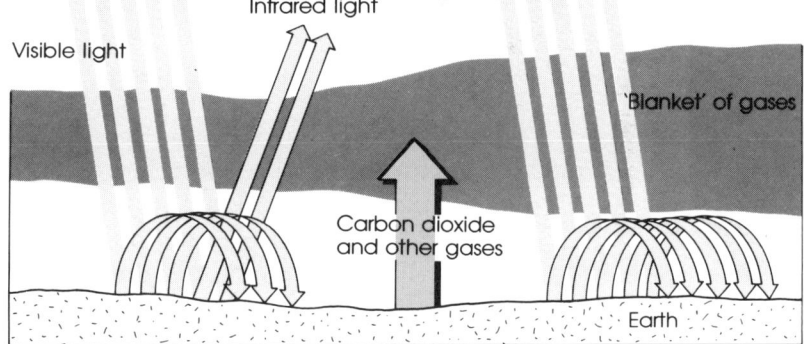

The 'blanket' of water vapour and carbon dioxide

The present situation
Visible light passes through the atmosphere to the Earth's surface. The Earth radiates heat as infrared rays. Some of this radiation escapes. Carbon dioxide and other gases in the lower atmosphere trap much of the radiation, thus keeping the Earth warm.

The future danger
The burning of fossil fuels and other processes add carbon dioxide, water vapour and other gases to the atmosphere. The thicker 'blanket' of gases prevents more of the infrared rays from escaping. The Earth is kept warmer than before.

Result The sea level rises. Low-lying areas are flooded.

Saving the rain forest

Another way of tackling the problem of the greenhouse effect is to stop cutting down forests. Plants take carbon dioxide out of the air in photosynthesis. In Brazil, the Amazon rain forest once covered 3 million square miles. Timber merchants have cut down 15% of the forest. Ranchers have cleared the land and planted grass. Cattle from South America feed the enormous US appetite for beef. The grasses planted for pasture survive for only 10 years before weeds take over. In the first year, one cow grazes about 2.5 acres; after 10 years it needs 17.5 acres. Without the roots of the trees to hold the soil in place, the tropical rain washes away the topsoil. Eventually torrential rain turns the land into eroded wasteland. Environmentalists have succeeded in stopping some hamburger chains from using South American beef. The enormous herds of cattle in South America do little to feed local people. British hamburgers are made from beef raised in the UK or the European Community. Corned beef from Brazil is sold in the UK. Mining companies have also cleared vast areas. When the felled trees are burned or left to rot, carbon dioxide and other greenhouse gases are released. Living trees take in carbon dioxide; felled trees produce carbon dioxide. The same kind of deforestation is going on in Central America, in some African countries, in India and in South-East Asia.

Many people in Europe are critical of Brazil for cutting down its rain forest. Brazil says that this is unfair, because Brazil needs to sell timber and beef to pay off its debts. Not all the people of Brazil benefit; the ranchers, the mining companies and the timber companies benefit. The native tribes who live in the Amazon rain forest are driven from their lands and herded into huts outside the forest, where they can no longer carry on their traditional way of life.

There are 155 000 species of flowering plants in tropical rain forests. Of these, 55 000 are in Brazil. One square mile of tropical rain forest contains about 380 species of flowering plants, 190 different trees and 40 different butterflies. If the present rate of destruction continues, by the middle of the twenty-first century 60 000 plant species will have become extinct. Some of the plants in the rain forest are sources of valuable drugs. A muscle relaxant, a treatment for glaucoma, a drug to relieve convulsions and drugs which treat cancer have been extracted from tropical plants. Only 2% of the world's flowering plants have so far been investigated for their medicinal properties. The forest clearance could wipe out plants which might hold a cure for cancer or AIDS.

Many people believe that the richer countries of the world should help Brazil to find a solution to the problem. Countries to which Brazil owes money could agree to cancel the debt in exchange for an area of rain forest. Brazil would then have to agree to leave that area of rain forest untouched in return for having the debt wiped out. This kind of arrangement has been called a *debt for nature exchange* or a *debt swap*. Conservation bodies have raised $5.4 million for conservation in Costa Rica, where every year 15 000 hectares of trees are planted. In one deal, 40 000 acres of tropical forest in Costa Rica were 'purchased' to be kept as a national park. In another deal, Conservation International cancelled a $650 000 debt owed by Bolivia when the Bolivian government agreed to protect 3.7 million acres of forest.

Commercial logging still consumes 12.5 million acres of tropical forest every year. Conservationists want to change the pattern of tree felling — to cut down only the number of trees that will be replaced naturally by young trees. There are other ways of raising money from forests. An area of 1200 acres planted with the fast-growing ipilipil tree could produce a million barrels of oil every year. In one year, a single Philippine petroleum nut tree produces 50 litres of oil used for heating and lighting.

The World Wide Fund for Nature (WWF) has made the defence of tropical rain forest its top priority. It is running 70 tropical forest projects around the world. In Cameroon in Africa, 126 000 hectares of tropical rain forest are kept as a national park. Scientists, working in a joint project with the Cameroon government and WWF, have extracted 90 chemical substances from plants, 38 of them new to science.

The World Bank has lent money to firms to invest in forest clearance. People of many countries believe that the World Bank should not do this. Without these loans, firms would not be able to buy the machinery they need to destroy tropical rain forests. The World Bank has been influenced by this criticism. It has cancelled or postponed funding of some projects. It has increased the number of staff in its environmental department from 2 to 60 people.

QUESTIONS ON THE GREENHOUSE EFFECT

1

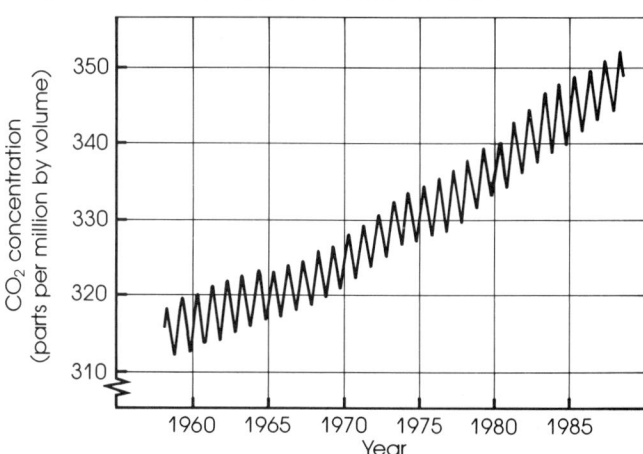

Carbon dioxide concentrations recorded at Mauna Loa Observatory in Hawaii

You can see that the concentration of carbon dioxide varies throughout the year.
(a) Does the level of carbon dioxide *production* change throughout the year? If it does, is it greater in winter or in summer? Explain your answer.

(b) Does the *absorption* of carbon dioxide change throughout the year? If it does, is it greater in winter or in summer? Explain your answer.
(c) What was the average concentration of carbon dioxide   (i) in 1960   (ii) in 1980?
(d) Work out an approximate figure for the percentage increase in carbon dioxide concentration from 1960 to 1980.

2 How can we reduce the level of carbon dioxide in the atmosphere? List as many ways as you can.

3 Britain buys a lot of tropical hardwoods. Friends of the Earth (FoE) publish *The Good Wood Guide* which tells whether or not tropical woods have been harvested in accordance with sound principles of forestry, at a rate which will not ruin the forest.

What do FoE mean by 'sound principles of forestry'? Why will these principles help to conserve forests?

4 The table gives figures for the demand for agricultural land and the area of forest remaining in the world. The figures for future years are estimates.

Year	Demand for agricultural land (million hectares)	Area of forest (million hectares)
1950	100	1145
1962	145	1000
1975	200	940
1987	375	830
2000	525	705
2012	690	515
2025	845	325

(a) On the same piece of graph paper, plot   (i) the demand for agricultural land and   (ii) the area of remaining forest, against the year.
(b) Suggest two ways in which the demand for agricultural land could be reduced.
(c) Explain why chopping down forests does not always increase the area of productive agricultural land.

MORE ABOUT PHOTOSYNTHESIS AND RESPIRATION

Plants absorb water through their roots. Their leaves take in carbon dioxide. Sunlight falls on to the leaves. Inside green plants, which contain the pigment chlorophyll, the process of photosynthesis takes place. Photosynthesis is the reaction:

$$\text{Carbon dioxide} + \text{Water} + \text{Energy of sunlight} \xrightarrow{\text{Chlorophyll}} \text{Sugar} + \text{Oxygen}$$

This is why plants take in carbon dioxide and give out oxygen. Where does the energy go? The energy, which comes from the Sun, is transformed by the plant into the energy of chemical bonds. These chemical bonds hold the atoms of carbon, hydrogen and oxygen in sugar together.

If many molecules of sugar join together, a molecule of starch is formed. Plants contain sugars and starches. Sugars and starches contain energy. When animals eat plants, they can use the energy contained in the sugars and starches.

Animals breathe in air which contains oxygen. In both animals and plants, the process of *respiration* occurs. Combustion of sugars in oxygen takes place.

Photosynthesis and respiration

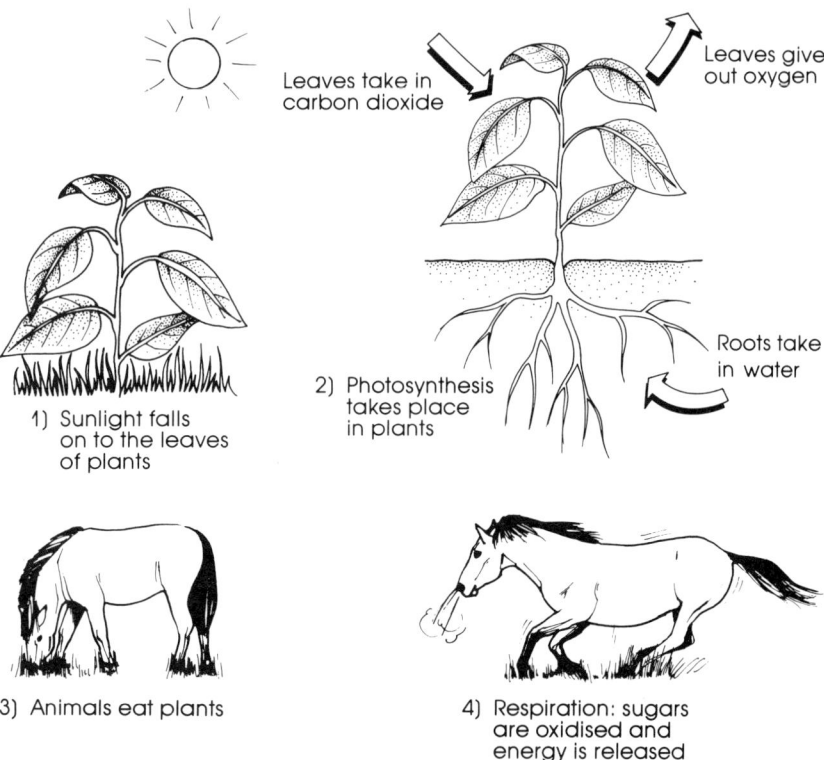

1) Sunlight falls on to the leaves of plants
2) Photosynthesis takes place in plants
Leaves take in carbon dioxide
Leaves give out oxygen
Roots take in water
3) Animals eat plants
4) Respiration: sugars are oxidised and energy is released

Carbon dioxide and water are formed. This is why animals breathe in air containing 21 per cent oxygen and 0.03 per cent carbon dioxide and breathe out air containing 16 per cent oxygen and 4 per cent carbon dioxide. The energy of the chemical bonds which held the atoms together in the sugar molecule is released. The equation for the chemical reaction which occurs in respiration is:

Sugar + Oxygen ⟶ Carbon dioxide + Water + Energy

The equation for respiration is the opposite of that for photosynthesis.

QUESTIONS ON CARBON DIOXIDE

Do not write on this page.

1 Supply a word or words to fill the blanks in the following passage.

Plants contain a green pigment called ____. It enables plants to make sugars. The materials which plants use to make sugars are ____ and ____. As well as sugars, ____ is formed. This plant process is called ____. In this process, plants use energy ____, and convert it into the energy ____ in the sugars. Plants convert sugars to ____ for storage. When we eat plants, we obtain ____ from the sugars and ____ they contain.

2 What is the percentage by volume of carbon dioxide in the air?

3 Some carbon dioxide dissolves in the sea. What do sea creatures do with this carbon dioxide? What happens to the sea creatures eventually? Does the carbon dioxide they use ever get back into the air?

4 What is the main process, other than dissolving in the sea, which removes carbon dioxide from the air? Why have people cut down forests in South America? What effect will this have on the amount of carbon dioxide in the air? Why are people worried about this?

5 Supply words to fill the blanks in this passage.

When plants decay, they are transformed by slow geological processes into ____. When this material burns, ____ and ____ are formed. When sea animals decay, they are transformed by slow geological processes into ____. When this material burns, ____ and ____ are formed.

CROSSWORD ON CARBON DIOXIDE

First, trace this grid on to a piece of paper (or photocopy this page). Then fill in the answers. Do not write on this page.

Across

1 This is formed during 11 across (5)
3 Plants _____ carbon dioxide for 11 across (3)
5 See 8 down
9 One time (4)
10 Quicklime is made in these (5)
11 The process in which plants turn carbon dioxide and water into sugars and oxygen (14)
12 Plants use these to take in water (5)
14 An 'electronic slave' (5)
15, 18 down   Oxygen comes _____ _____ plant leaves (3, 2)
16 In desert lands, soil can be worn away by _____ (7)
19 See 2 down
21 It burns to form carbon dioxide and water (3)
22 If you cover up the leaves of a plant it will make less _____ (6)
23 See 20 down

Down

2, 19 across   The action of carbon dioxide in keeping the Earth warm has been called this (10, 6)
4 You must have this for 11 across to take place (8)
5 The process in which animals turn sugars and oxygen into carbon dioxide and water (11)
6 The green pigment in plants (11)
7 On your own (4)
8, 5 across   These are formed over many thousands of years from the shells of millions of dead sea creatures (9, 5)
13 Sea creatures make theirs from calcium compounds (6)
17 _____ plants run out of carbon dioxide we shall run out of food (2)
18 See 15 across
20, 23 across   It dissolves carbon dioxide (3, 3)

THE NOBLE GASES

The noble gases are helium, neon, argon, krypton and xenon. They are very unreactive. For a long time, it was believed that they did not take part in any chemical reactions at all.

Helium has an extremely low density. It is used to fill balloons sent up for weather research. Hydrogen is an even less dense gas, but it forms an explosive mixture with air. Helium is one of the least reactive elements known, and helium balloons are therefore safer than hydrogen balloons.

Deep-sea divers need oxygen. If they use oxygen mixed with nitrogen, nitrogen dissolves in their blood. At the high pressures they experience in deep water, nitrogen is very soluble. When the divers surface, nitrogen is less soluble than it was at high pressure. It comes out of solution in the blood, and, as it does so, it gives the divers severe pains called 'the bends'. If the oxygen is mixed with helium, helium does not dissolve, and there is no danger of 'the bends'.

Neon lights for advertising

Neon and argon are used in artificial lights. If an electrical discharge is passed through these gases at low pressure, they emit a glow. Since they are chemically unreactive, neon and argon never become used up inside a light tube. Neon lights are famous for their brightness and their long life. Argon is used in electric light bulbs.

A one-man submersible used for commercial diving

SOME EXPERIMENTS ON AIR

Here are some suggestions for experiments on air. If you are interested, ask your teacher to give you full instructions.

EXPERIMENT 1

Some experiments on photosynthesis

Many books on biology and general science have directions for experiments which will help you to answer these questions.

How do you test for starch?
How do you test a leaf for starch?
Where is starch formed in a variegated (two-tone) leaf?
Is light needed for the formation of starch?
Is carbon dioxide needed for the formation of starch?
Do plants give out oxygen?
Can respiration take place in the absence of air?

EXPERIMENT 2

Measure your lung power

The diagram below shows a boy breathing out into a Winchester bottle full of water. The volume of water he displaces from the bottle is equal to the volume of air expelled from his lungs.

Can you see how he could use the same apparatus to find out what volume of air he can suck in?

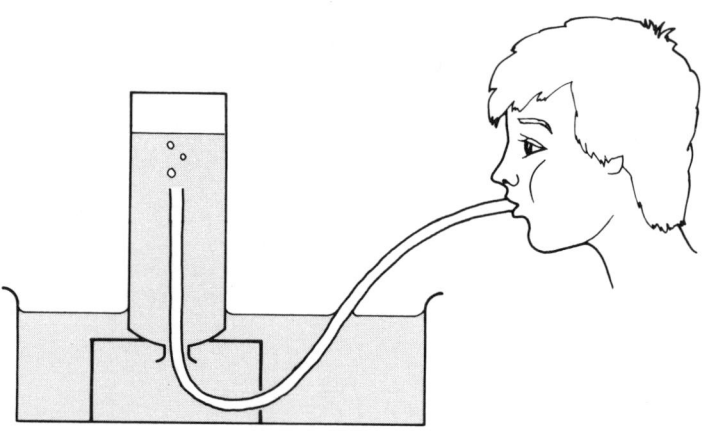

EXPERIMENT 3

What volume of air passes through your lungs in 24 hours?

The diagram below shows a girl breathing out into a measuring cylinder. She breathes in through her nose, and out through her mouth. She times how long it takes to fill the measuring cylinder. Then she calculates what volume she would breathe out if she went on for 24 hours.

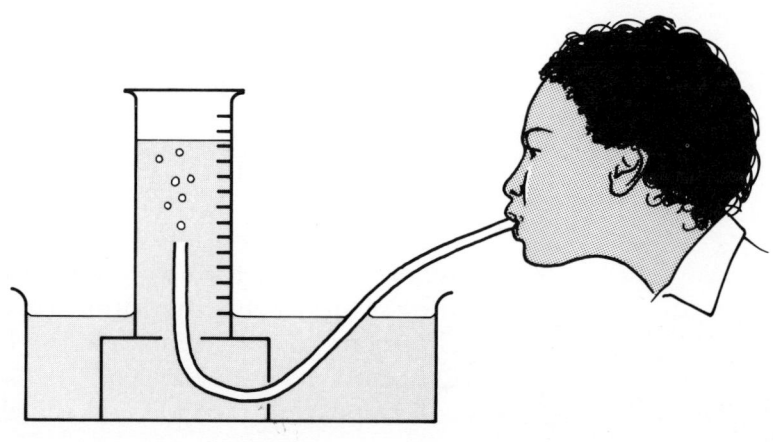

EXPERIMENT 4

Does the air you breathe out contain more carbon dioxide than ordinary air?

The girl shown in the diagram has filled a plastic bottle with water. She is using her breath to displace the water. When she has a full bottle, she will squeeze the bottle, as shown, to drive the air into limewater. Next, she fills the bottle with ordinary air and squeezes this into some more limewater. Which will turn the limewater milky?

EXPERIMENT 5

How do clouds form?

If you do the experiment shown in the diagram below, you will be able to say in which beaker clouds form fastest. This will tell you something about cloud formation.

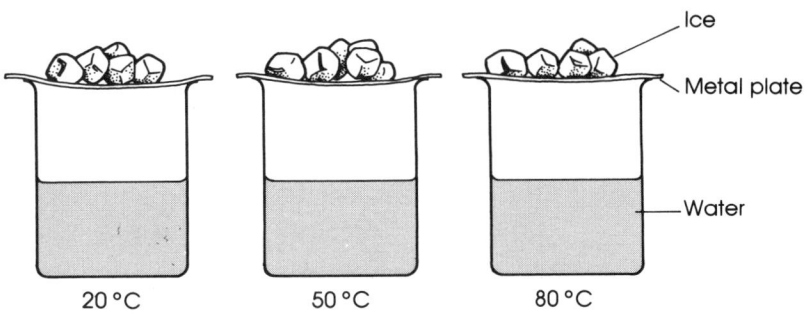

CHAPTER 2 POLLUTANTS

WHAT ARE POLLUTANTS?

The gases we have studied so far are useful gases. There are, however, pollutants in the air. Industries burn fuels which put pollutants into the air. Cars and lorries burn petrol and send out pollutant gases through their exhausts. Any substance which is damaging to health is called a pollutant. The chief pollutants present in the air are shown below. They are:

Smoke

Smoke consists of tiny solid particles of carbon and unburnt fuel. The particles are about 1 μm across (a millionth of a metre, 10^{-6} m).

Grit and Dust

Grit and dust are made up of those parts of fuels that will not burn. The particles are larger than smoke. Grit particles are about 100 μm across, and dust particles about 10 μm.

Fog

Fog consists of tiny droplets of water and particles of sulphur.

Sulphur Dioxide

Sulphur dioxide is sent into the air when fuels containing sulphur are burnt.

Carbon Monoxide

Carbon monoxide is obtained from the incomplete combustion of petrol and diesel oil.

Other Pollutants

Present in smaller amounts are lead compounds, which come from petrol-driven vehicle exhausts. Fluorides are found in the air in the neighbourhood of brick-works. Mercury compounds and mercury vapour are sometimes present in polluted air. Nitrogen oxides—nitrogen dioxide, NO_2, and nitrogen monoxide, NO—are also pollutants. They come from car and lorry exhausts. In moist air, they form the strong acid, nitric acid. This causes unpleasant irritation of the eyes and throat and damage to buildings.

Pollutants make our environment less pleasant and less safe. They make people and buildings dirty. They make city air dark by scattering and also absorbing sunlight. Plants suffer from a lack of light and from poisoning by pollutant gases. Inner city areas come to lack plants and trees. Buildings become grimy and then start to crumble as they are attacked by sulphur dioxide. City dwellers breathe in pollutant gases and develop diseases in the lungs and throat.

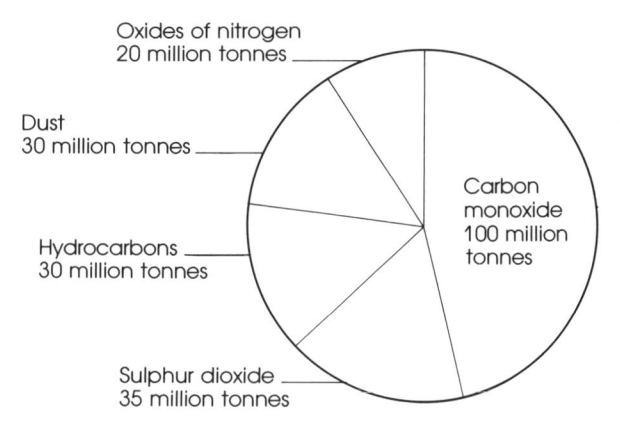

The pollutants produced in the United Kingdom in a year

- Oxides of nitrogen 20 million tonnes
- Dust 30 million tonnes
- Hydrocarbons 30 million tonnes
- Sulphur dioxide 35 million tonnes
- Carbon monoxide 100 million tonnes

All this costs money. The damage to buildings has to be repaired. The damage to crops in polluted areas costs money. When workers are absent through ill health, the productivity of their factory or business drops. All these factors add up. Pollution costs the United Kingdom between £350 million and £500 million a year.

Let us have a look at what some pollutant gases do.

SMOG: THE SILENT KILLER

The word *smog* was coined in 1952. It means a mixture of smoke and fog. The word was new in 1952, but the problem was not. London had suffered from smog for 100 years. Londoners called their smogs 'pea-soupers' when they were really dense and yellowish-green.

Fog consists of water droplets. It is formed when warm air containing water vapour is suddenly cooled. The air can no longer hold all the water vapour that it could hold when it was warm, and water condenses out. The air is damp with droplets of water. Fog soon clears away in a wind, but on a still day it will hang around. Fog is dangerous because we cannot see through it. When there is fog on the motorways, we hear of accidents. Unless motorists drive very slowly, they cannot see far enough ahead to brake in time to avoid hitting the car in front.

If fog is mixed with smoke, there is another danger. Smoke contains irritating particles of ash. Fog prevents smoke escaping into the upper atmosphere. Smoke hangs around, and we breathe it in. It irritates our lungs and makes us cough. Smoke also contains the gas sulphur dioxide (SO_2). This gas dissolves in water to form a weak acid called sulphurous acid (H_2SO_3). Oxygen in the air combines with sulphurous acid to form sulphuric acid (H_2SO_4), which is a strong acid. When we breathe in smog, we are breathing in droplets of sulphuric acid. It is a strong acid and irritates our lungs. Our lungs react by forming a lot of mucus, which we cough up.

In London, during the winter of 1951–2, there was a smog which lasted for 5 days. No wind came along to disperse the fog. In the centre of the city the fog was heavily polluted—a real 'smog'. Chimneys continued to belch out more pollution into the fog. Drivers could not see through the smog to deliver supplies of milk, bread and coal. Pedestrians got lost in the fog and sometimes walked round in circles for hours, trying to find their way home. Thousands of people became ill through breathing in polluted air, and 3000 died. The reason for their deaths was that they had breathed in too much sulphur dioxide.

After the 1952 smog and the terrible number of deaths, Parliament took stock of the situation. In 1956, there was another 'killer smog', and in the same year Parliament passed the *Clean Air Act*. This stopped people burning fuels which produced dark smoke, and created *smokeless zones*. In these

London smog

zones, the only fuels which could be burned were those that contain a smaller amount of sulphur than average and produce less smoke than average (low-smoke and low-sulphur fuels). These fuels are often called *smokeless fuels*.

Why do we burn fuels which contain sulphur? We burn petrol in cars and diesel oil in buses and lorries. All these put sulphur dioxide into the air. Factories burn coal and oil, and their chimneys put sulphur dioxide into the air. But there is a cure. Oil can be refined to take out sulphur compounds. Some people have paraffin stoves burning in their homes. The paraffin that they burn is obtained by distillation of petroleum oil. It is carefully purified to remove sulphur compounds. As you can imagine, people could not bear to have sulphur dioxide pouring into their houses, so they are prepared to pay more for a sulphur-free fuel. Petrol could be purified in the same way, but it would be more expensive. If one oil company did this, and not the rest, its petrol would be dearer than that of other companies. Do you think people would buy the dearer petrol to avoid polluting the air?

We have to think carefully about what clean air is worth to us. Is it worth a few pence on every gallon of petrol the motorist buys? Polluted air costs us money. It costs money to treat all the people who suffer from breathing troubles (such as bronchitis and asthma). People who are away from work with breathing difficulties cost money in that the productivity of their offices and factories drops. Sulphur dioxide eats away buildings, and costly maintenance work has to be done to preserve them. At the same time as we are passing this dangerous gas into the air, we are actually paying to import sulphur from other countries. We need it to make the important chemical sulphuric acid.

PHOTOCHEMICAL SMOG

Other nations have their problems too. Japan is a crowded little country. Factories, homes, cars and lorries burn petroleum oil and pass sulphur dioxide into the air. In 1970, the people of Tokyo suffered from an outbreak of smarting eyes and sore throats. It was so bad that Tokyo Radio advised people to stay inside. The cause of this kind of pollution is a chemical reaction which needs three things. These are:
    (1) hydrocarbons (compounds of hydrogen and carbon) from the exhausts of cars and lorries;
    (2) nitrogen oxides (of formulae NO and NO_2), also from vehicle exhausts; and
    (3) intense sunlight.

In intense sunlight, the oxides of nitrogen combine with hydrocarbons. This reaction produces compounds which are irritating to the eyes and throat.

This kind of pollution is called *photochemical smog*. (The word 'photo' comes from the Greek word for 'light'.) The solution to the smog problem is to cut down the number of cars sending their exhaust fumes into the city air. Car pools and more public transport would help. Running cars and buses on a fuel other than petrol would be a real solution. Research is being carried out on running cars on propane, natural gas and electrical batteries.

TEMPERATURE INVERSION: LOS ANGELES

Hot air rises. Normally, air is warm near the ground. It rises, taking pollution with it, and cold air takes its place.

In Los Angeles, on the west coast of the United States, a different situation arises. The hot Sun produces a layer of air above the city which is warmer than the city air. There is a temperature inversion. Warm air is on top of cooler air. The city air cannot rise because it is cooler than the air above it. As the day wears on, photochemical smog is formed, and eyes and throats become sore.

A temperature inversion

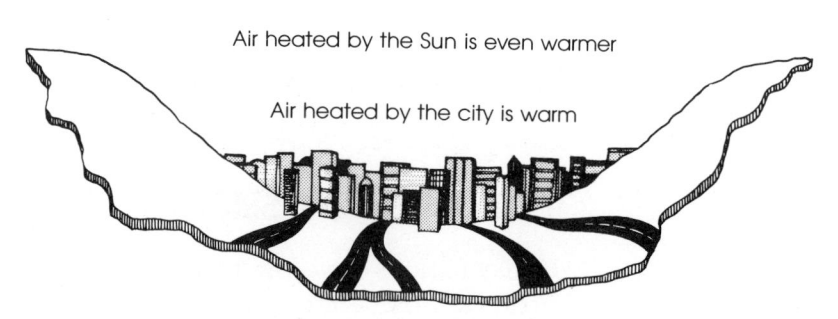

Air heated by the Sun is even warmer

Air heated by the city is warm

There is a danger of a temperature inversion in places which have a hot climate and still air. A low-lying area surrounded by higher ground tends to have still air.

SULPHUR DIOXIDE STRIKES AGAIN: THE ACROPOLIS

The Acropolis is one of the most beautiful groups of buildings in the world. It stands on a huge limestone hill overlooking the city of Athens in Greece. Five centuries before the birth of Christ, the citizens of Athens built the Acropolis. It was a fortified inner city, which could be defended against attackers. The most important building in it was the great marble temple, the Parthenon, dedicated to their goddess, Athena.

The Parthenon

The Acropolis has overlooked the city of Athens for 24 centuries. All this time, people have never got tired of looking at it. Fashions in beauty and architecture have changed, but the Acropolis has never gone out of style. People have journeyed from all over the world to admire the proportions of the buildings, the simplicity of the great marble columns and the grace of the statues. Travellers have been known to burst into tears, overcome by the beauty of the sight. At night, the Acropolis is illuminated and shines out over Athens.

The ancient Greeks used small iron bolts and clamps in their architecture. They made the iron almost rustproof by coating it with lead. When repairs were made in the nineteenth century, steel bolts were used. These have now rusted, and, in rusting, have expanded and cracked the marble. At present, repair workers are replacing the rusty steel bolts with rods of titanium, a metal which does not corrode.

Now, after surviving for 24 centuries, the Acropolis is in danger. The industries of modern Athens are sending sulphur dioxide into the air. Car exhausts and central heating furnaces are giving out sulphur dioxide. If there is any moisture in the air, sulphur dioxide dissolves to form the weak acid, sulphurous acid. Oxygen in the air oxidises this to the strong acid, sulphuric acid. Sulphuric acid attacks marble to form calcium sulphate. This substance is plaster-like. (Plaster of Paris is a form of calcium sulphate.) Soot and dust stick to it to form a grimy crust. The slow weathering of the Acropolis has speeded up in the last 25 years. As calcium sulphate dissolves slowly in rain, the marble columns are beginning to crumble. The statues carved so lovingly by craftsmen long ago are losing their delicate outlines. Details of face and hair are becoming blurred as the acid eats into the marble. The photograph below shows the Caryatids, a group of graceful statues which support the roof of one of the temples.

The people of Athens want to save their beautiful Acropolis. The danger from sulphur dioxide was something they did not foresee as the modern city developed. To save the Acropolis, the real solution is to move cars and factories out of the city. To do this, Athenians will have to undertake a huge rebuilding programme. All this will take time. They plan to build a ring

The Caryatids

road to speed the movement of traffic around the city and to keep out heavy commercial vehicles. New factories will be built outside the city.

More immediate measures have been taken. The Government have banned the construction of tall buildings near the Acropolis. They have banned the use of the high-sulphur oil (called mazout) which was burnt in central heating systems. Industrial pollution has been cut by a third. Drivers are allowed to use their cars only on alternate weeks (according to whether the car carries an odd or even number plate). The centre of the city is closed to cars. Shops have been made to stay open at midday to reduce the number of rush hours from four to two. The Caryatids have been removed to the Acropolis Museum, and copies are being made to take their place until the atmosphere improves.

ACID RAIN

Sulphur dioxide (SO_2) and nitrogen dioxide (NO_2) are produced by electricity-generating plants and by industrial plants. Tall chimneys take the acid gases up into the air, where they are caught up by the wind and taken far away from the factory workers and their homes. They are out of sight and out of mind, but, unfortunately, not for ever. The gases react with water vapour and oxygen to form a dilute solution of sulphuric acid (H_2SO_4) and nitric acid (HNO_3). Eventually, the water vapour and its acid content become captured by a cloud, and finally fall as *acid rain* or *acid snow*. This may turn up days later and hundreds of miles away.

How pollution travels

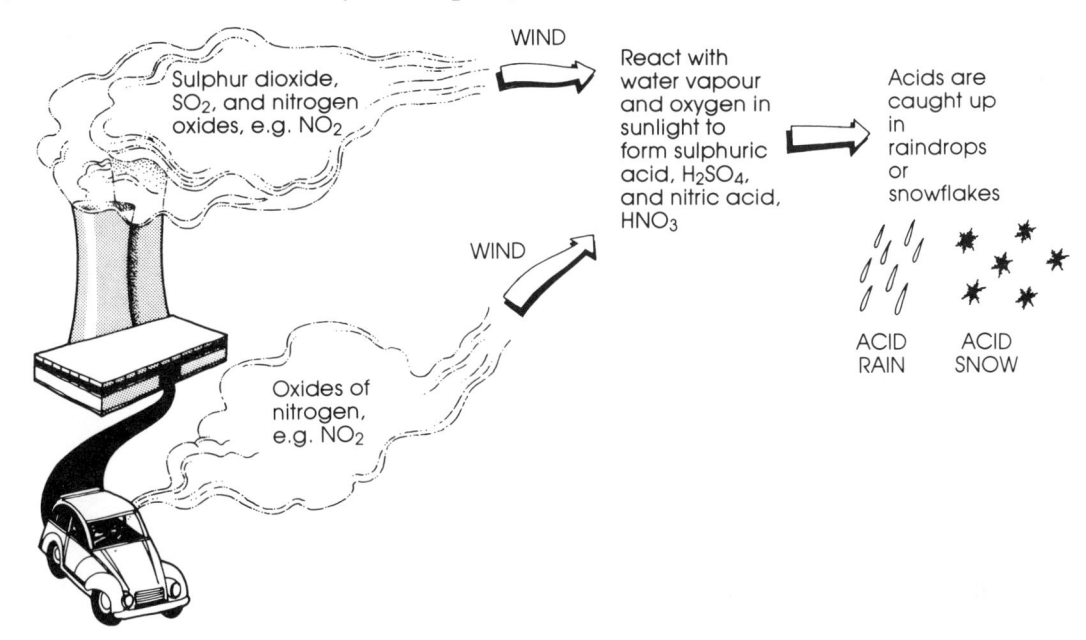

Sulphur dioxide, SO_2, and nitrogen oxides, e.g. NO_2

WIND

React with water vapour and oxygen in sunlight to form sulphuric acid, H_2SO_4, and nitric acid, HNO_3

Acids are caught up in raindrops or snowflakes

WIND

Oxides of nitrogen, e.g. NO_2

ACID RAIN   ACID SNOW

All rain is slightly acidic. Unpolluted rain-water contains carbonic acid, because carbon dioxide dissolves in it, and nitric acid in small concentrations. Rain which is more acidic than natural rain-water is described as *acid rain*. In 1978 an exceptionally bad rainfall fell on Kane, Pennsylvania in the United States. It was as acidic as vinegar, 1000 times more acidic than pure rain.

What are the effects of acid rain? On land, it is absorbed into the soil. It reacts with minerals containing compounds of calcium, potassium, aluminium and other metals, and converts the metals into soluble salts. The solution of salts in rain-water trickles into the deeper layers of the soil. Salts are removed from the topsoil, where tree roots are trying to obtain them for nourishment. The acid rain-water containing the salts meets rock, and makes its way along the bedrock into lakes and rivers. The lakes become more and more acidic, and concentrations of metal salts in the lake-water build up. Fish pass water over their gills in order to extract oxygen and salts. Aluminium compounds (e.g. aluminium hydroxide) come out of solution and are deposited on the gills. The fish secrete mucus to try to combat the deposit. The gills become clogged with mucus and aluminium hydroxide, and the fish die.

Salmon have disappeared from the lakes of southern Norway, and trout have gone from 2000 lakes. Sweden has 100 000 lakes. Of these, 9000 are now poorly stocked with fish, and 4000 lakes are dead. Lime has been sprayed on to 1000 lakes to neutralise the acidic water. One reason why Norway and

Acid rain affects trees and fish

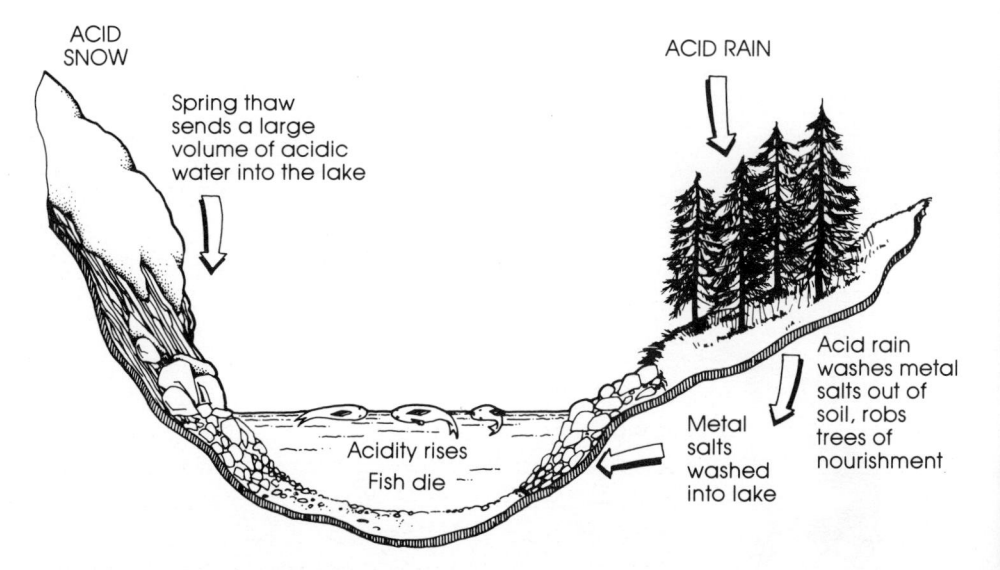

ACID SNOW

Spring thaw sends a large volume of acidic water into the lake

ACID RAIN

Acid rain washes metal salts out of soil, robs trees of nourishment

Metal salts washed into lake

Acidity rises
Fish die

Acidity is reduced if the rocks contain limestone, which neutralises acids

Sweden suffer badly is that snow piles up during the hard winter. In the spring thaw, the winter's accumulation of acid snow washes straight into the lakes. The slow passage through soil and over rock, during which rain is partly neutralised, does not take place. The lakes suffer a sudden increase in acidity, and the fish die.

Norway and Sweden do not have power stations belching out sulphur dioxide. They use their waterfalls to produce hydroelectric power. The pollution in Scandinavia comes from the United Kingdom and West Germany. Swedish schoolchildren recently started a protest campaign. They sent thousands of postcards to the West German government, protesting that acid rain falling on their country is coming from the industries of the Rühr in West Germany. The amount coming from the United Kingdom is less, as most of it falls into the North Sea. Nevertheless, the United Kingdom is exporting pollution to friendly neighbouring countries.

The United Kingdom is affected too. Rivers and lakes in Scotland are being treated with lime to reduce acidity and revive stocks of fish. The Lake District farmers too are complaining that acid rain is spoiling their fishing.

Forests, also, have been affected. In the mid-1970s, Alpine forests started to lose their fir trees. In the famous Black Forest of Germany, spruce trees began to turn brown and lose their needles. Surveys in The Netherlands, Czechoslovakia, Switzerland and the UK have shown that 20 to 30 per cent of trees have lost a large fraction of their leaves. Acidic rainwater washes nutrients out of the soils. Without essential nutrients, trees suffer poor growth, become unhealthy and may die.

What has acid rain to do with your skiing holiday? In 1987, Herr Gunter, leader of the Independence Party in Switzerland, claimed that skiers in Swiss resorts face increasing danger from avalanches. The reason is that forests are being killed off. In some Swiss forests, 80 per cent of the trees are dying or dead. The trees which used to divert avalanches are no longer there to hold back the snow.

In 1987, the UK Forestry Commission reported on the health of trees. They said that 40–60 per cent of mature oak trees in the UK had lost more than one-quarter of their leaves. Of Norway spruce trees, which are used commercially, over 75 per cent had lost more than one-quarter of their leaves. The health of trees has worsened rapidly since 1985. The Commission has not come to any conclusion about the cause of the rapid deterioration of trees.

Acid rain attacks metallic structures, e.g. bridges, ships and motor vehicles. Building materials, such as limestone, sandstone, cement and concrete are also attacked.

In 1979, 31 European countries, including the United Kingdom, signed an agreement called the Convention on Long Range Transboundary Air Pollution. Each nation promised to stop exporting pollution. All nations committed themselves to act with consideration for the environments of other countries.

In 1980, the United States and Canada signed a similar agreement to reduce the emission of sulphur dioxide and nitrogen dioxide. The United States, Canada and Europe together put 100 million tonnes of sulphur dioxide into the air each year. Industrialists have not yet put into practice the measures on which their governments agreed, but a start has been made.

Statue attacked by pollution

What can be done to reduce the sulphur dioxide emission? There are three main measures.

(1) Low-sulphur fuels would help. The coal used in power stations contains 1 to 2 per cent sulphur. By crushing and washing with a suitable solvent, from 10 to 40 per cent of the sulphur can be removed. Oil-fired power stations are worse, but oil refineries can produce oils with a lower sulphur content. It is more costly, and the price of electricity would be higher. To compensate for this, there would be less damage to lakes, crops and buildings. A new technique called *coal gasification* converts coal into a gaseous fuel. The sulphur in the coal is

converted into sulphur dioxide and hydrogen sulphide, which can be removed from the fuel.

(2) New burners have been invented. Coal can be burnt in a bed of limestone (calcium carbonate, $CaCO_3$). This decomposes to form calcium oxide (CaO). This base combines with the acidic oxides of sulphur and nitrogen. This type of combustion is called *pulverised fluidised bed combustion,* PFBC ('pulverised' because the coal is ground; 'fluidised' because the bed of limestone is in constant motion as gases move through it). PFBC is being adopted by many pollution-conscious countries.

(3) Acid gases can be removed from the chimneys. After the coal or oil has been burnt, the combustion products, including the acid gases, start up the chimney. Jets of wet lime bombard the combustion gases and neutralise the acid gases to form a sludge. This method is called *flue gas desulphurisation,* FGD. It can remove up to 95 per cent of the acid gases before they leave the chimney.

The Central Electricity Generating Board (CEGB) of the UK has been slow to spend money on desulphurisation. In 1988, Prince Charles said, 'I would have thought that the CEGB was doing too little and too late. Our responsibilities do lie in not exporting our problems abroad'. The Prince suggested that on attitudes to the environment many industries were out of step with 'the ordinary bloke'.

Drax Power station in Yorkshire is Western Europe's largest coal-fired power station. The CEGB has announced plans to spend £400 million on a FGD plant for Drax power station. This will remove 90 per cent of the sulphur dioxide discharged from the power station. The waste product will be calcium sulphate (gypsum). Some of the gypsum will be sold to the plasterboard industry and to cement manufacturers. The Drax power station FGD plant will start working in stages between 1993–95.

One solution to the problem of pollution from coal and oil is to switch to nuclear power stations. These have their dangers too (see pp. 63–5 and also Extending Science 9: *Nuclear Power*). France and West Germany obtain much of their electricity from nuclear power stations. Another solution is to harness *renewable energy sources,* e.g. wind, waves, tides, waterfalls and solar energy. These alternative energy sources do not give rise to pollution (see Extending Science 7: *Energy*). Switzerland and Norway obtain electricity from hydroelectric power stations which employ waterfalls.

QUESTIONS ON SULPHUR AND ACID RAIN

1. The table gives figures for $\dfrac{\text{mass of sulphur deposited}}{\text{mass of sulphur emitted}} \times 100\%$.

Country	Sulphur deposited as a percentage of sulphur emitted
Austria	219
Belgium	56
Bulgaria	76
Denmark	59
East Germany	43
Finland	166
Hungary	61
Ireland	127
Italy	62
Norway	527
Portugal	178
Sweden	234
Switzerland	238
UK	45
USSR	143
West Germany	67
Yugoslavia	72

   (a) List the countries which import pollution—receive more pollution than they produce. (Finland is one: it receives 1.66 times as much pollution as it produces.)
   (b) List the countries which export pollution—receive less pollution than they produce.
   (c) Name the two biggest importers of pollution and the two biggest exporters of pollution.
   (d) Show the figures for the countries which you listed in part (a) as a bar chart.
   (e) Show the figures for the countries which you listed in part (b) as a bar chart.

2. Which building materials, concrete, brick, sandstone, limestone etc., are most at risk of damage by acid rain? Describe an investigation you could do in a school laboratory to answer this question. Say what you would do. List the apparatus you would use. Say what you would look for. (*Hint:* You can make sulphur dioxide in the laboratory by adding an acid to sodium sulphite or sodium metabisulphite.)

3 The table gives the annual emission of sulphur (in tonnes per 1000 inhabitants) for a number of countries.

Country	Sulphur emission in tonnes per 1000 inhabitants
Portugal	10
Turkey	21
Switzerland	21
Norway	28
Netherlands	35
Ireland	37
Spain	48
Austria	49
Sweden	58
Greece	64
France	66
West Germany	66
Belgium	68
Italy	79
Denmark	80
Romania	82
UK	83
Finland	89
Poland	102
USSR	103
Bulgaria	123
Hungary	172
Yugoslavia	178
Czechoslovakia	213
East Germany	251

(a) Show these figures as a bar chart.
(b) Which part of Europe do the major polluters occupy?
(c) Suggest a reason why these countries have such a big problem.
(d) Suggest a reason why Portugal does not produce much pollution.
(e) Switzerland and Norway are industrialised countries, with a high demand for electricity.
How do they get the electricity they need without producing as much sulphur as some of the other countries?
(f) France and West Germany are both highly industrialised countries. Other countries produce a lot more pollution.
How do France and West Germany get the electricity they need while producing less sulphur than many other industrial nations?

AEROSOLS AND THE OZONE LAYER: PUSH-BUTTON CONVENIENCE OR PUSH-BUTTON CANCER?

Oxygen molecules have the formula O_2. This shows that there are two atoms in each molecule. Ozone has the formula O_3, showing that there are three oxygen atoms in a molecule of ozone. Ozone is formed from oxygen when oxygen absorbs energy from ultraviolet rays. This is why there is a layer of ozone surrounding the Earth. It is at a distance of 25 kilometres (15 miles) from the surface of the Earth.

The ozone layer cuts out some of the ultraviolet light coming from the Sun. This is a good thing because ultraviolet light is bad for us and can cause skin cancer. In Australia, where sunlight is intense, people who are out in the Sun a lot develop skin cancers. In addition, ultraviolet radiation can cause eye cataracts, can damage the genes of all living things and can reduce crop yields. If the Earth lost the protection of the ozone layer, it would be uninhabitable.

Ozone is a very reactive element. It will react with a large number of chemicals, forming oxygen in the process. When the upper atmosphere becomes polluted, ozone oxidises the pollutants and the ozone layer becomes thinner, giving us less protection from the ultraviolet light.

There are two pollutants that people are worried about. One is the material in aerosol cans. Aerosol cans contain the substance which is to be sprayed and a *propellant*. The propellant is a liquid which can easily be turned to gas by releasing the pressure on it. When you press the button, a valve opens, and the propellant vaporises. It comes out of the nozzle carrying the useful liquid with it. The useful liquid may be shoe polish, window cleaner, paint, oven cleaner, shaving cream, etc. Spraying is a very quick and convenient method of applying all these liquids. The propellant is likely to be a CFC (a chlorofluorohydrocarbon).

For many years, manufacturers have been delighted with these useful liquids. Because they are chemically unreactive, they never corrode any materials they are used on. CFCs are also used as the cooling liquids in refrigerators and air conditioners, as the blowing agents in making foam insulation and as solvents for cleaning microelectronic circuits. There is a drawback to these marvellous compounds. Now people are keen to get rid of CFCs because of their action on the ozone layer.

CFCs are very, very stable compounds. They enter the air and meet nothing which can destroy them. They drift up and up into the atmosphere, for miles and miles, until they meet the ozone layer. At last, they have found something that can react with them. Ozone oxidises the CFCs and, in doing so, forms oxygen. When this happens the ozone layer becomes a little thinner.

Another pollutant that is likely to be found at this distance from the Earth is the exhaust fumes from high-flying aeroplanes, such as Concorde. The exhaust gases contain nitrogen monoxide (formula NO). Some ozone is used up in oxidising this gas to nitrogen dioxide (formula NO_2).

For many years, scientists suspected that CFCs might attack the ozone layer. In 1982, a team of British scientists found evidence that it was actually happening. Joe Farman and his team were taking measurements at the British Antarctic Survey Station in the Antarctic. They used an instrument called a *spectrophotometer*. It measures light and analyses it into different wavelengths. By detecting light sent out by ozone, the spectrophotometer is able to measure the amount of

Concorde

ozone in the atmosphere. In the spring of 1982, Joe Farman was studying a set of spectrophotometer readings. He was amazed to find a big decrease in the ozone layer over the Antarctic. About 20% of the ozone seemed to have disappeared. Farman studied the results carefully and checked the spectrophotometer for faults. He could see no reason to doubt the results. There was a reason why Farman was so careful in coming to conclusions. A US satellite was orbiting over the Antarctic and passing information on the ozone layer to the US Space Flight Centre. Why had the Americans not seen the thinning of the ozone layer? Farman was mystified. When Farman announced his team's discovery, it was the Americans' turn to be surprised. The American computers had been programmed to record small changes in the ozone layer and reject any incredibly large changes. Since this date, the US has carried out a $10 million research programme. High-flying planes have been fitted with instruments and used to collect data on the atmosphere at a height of 20 km. These data help us to understand what is attacking the ozone layer. The instruments have detected breakdown products of CFCs in the upper atmosphere.

In March, 1989, a team of scientists working in the Canadian Arctic detected a 'hole' (really a thinning) in the ozone layer over the Arctic. This is even more serious than the 'hole' over the Antarctic. It means that some of the most populated parts of the globe, including North America, northern Europe and the Soviet Union, will have less protection from ultraviolet radiation. The effects could include an increase in skin cancers and eye cataracts, danger to marine life, reduced crop yields and an increase in the Earth's temperature.

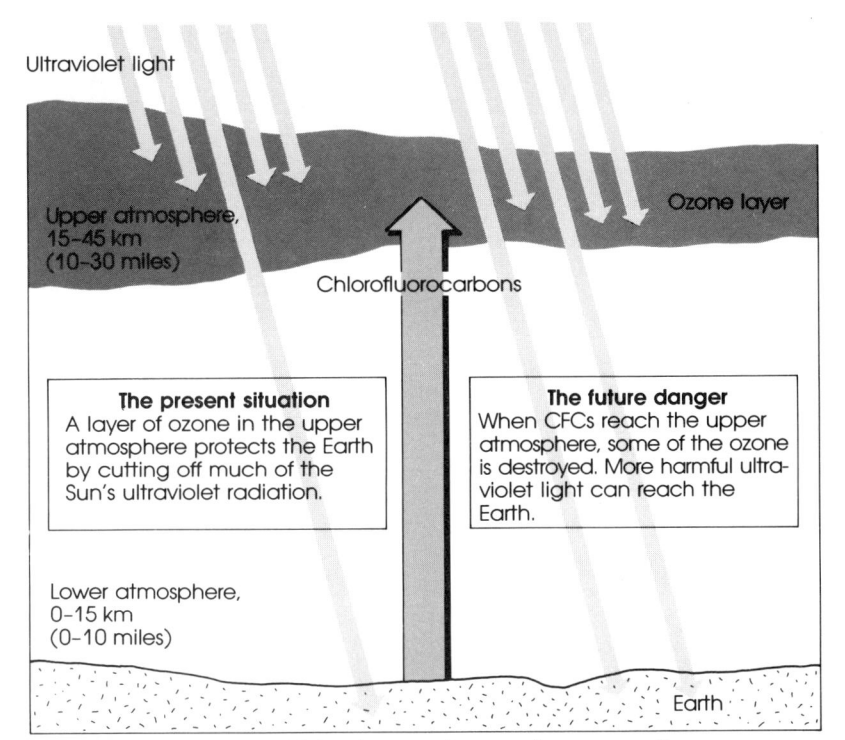

Thinning of the ozone layer

Ultraviolet light

Upper atmosphere, 15–45 km (10–30 miles)

Ozone layer

Chlorofluorocarbons

The present situation A layer of ozone in the upper atmosphere protects the Earth by cutting off much of the Sun's ultraviolet radiation.

The future danger When CFCs reach the upper atmosphere, some of the ozone is destroyed. More harmful ultra-violet light can reach the Earth.

Lower atmosphere, 0–15 km (0–10 miles)

Earth

What could happen Higher temperatures make some northern countries more fertile. Some southern countries become dust-bowls. Skin cancer and eye cataracts increase.

Saving the ozone layer

What can we do to save the ozone layer? In September, 1987, 38 nations signed an agreement called the Montreal Protocol. This was an agreement to reduce their use of CFCs by 50% by the year 2000. In London in March, 1989, 124 nations met to discuss how to save the ozone layer. The UK and other countries pledged to cut the use of CFCs by 85% by the year 2000. The European Community promised to ban CFCs completely by the year 2000. A number of countries have not signed the Montreal agreement. China, with one-fifth of the world's population, accounts for only 1% of the total CFC usage. However, China is planning to put refrigerators into 15% of homes by the end of the century. That would mean 200 million fridges, loaded with CFCs. India and Brazil make up another one-fifth of the world's population. To persuade the people of China, India, Brazil and other developing countries not to manufacture and use CFCs will be difficult. Substitutes for CFCs are more expensive. Developing countries are likely to resent being told not to use CFCs by industrialised countries which have used CFCs for 40 years.

The chemical industry is looking for substitutes for CFCs. In aerosols, liquefied hydrocarbons, such as propane, can be used. They have the disadvantage of being flammable. In 1987

McDonald's food chain said that it was doing its bit to preserve the ozone layer. The company changed the plastic foam packages it uses to keep food hot to a foam which is made with hydrocarbons. Other fast food chains did the same.

QUESTIONS ON THE OZONE LAYER

1 Early in 1988, Prince Charles banned aerosols from his household. Since that time, many nations have agreed to cut down their use of CFCs and a large number of manufacturers have stopped using CFCs in aerosols.
   (a) Make a list of personal products and household products that are sold in aerosol cans.
   (b) Say how these products could be packaged without using aerosols.
   (c) Say what advantages aerosol cans have over the alternative packaging. Say how important (or otherwise) these advantages are.
   (d) You may like to form a group to tackle this survey.
   - Look on the shelves of your local pharmacist and supermarket.
   - Make a list of products which are now sold in 'ozone-friendly' or 'environment-friendly' aerosol cans.
   - Make a list of products which are now sold in pump-action cans or bottles.
   - Which do you think is better: an 'ozone-friendly' aerosol or a pump-action can? Give your reasons.
   (e) People who insist on buying products which do not damage the environment are called 'green' consumers. Why are they described as 'green'? What products other than CFC aerosol cans would green consumers avoid? This is a big question; perhaps you would like to form a group to discuss it.

2 Give *two* advantages of the traditional cardboard egg-box over the foam plastic egg-box.

3 CFCs are used in refrigerators.
   (a) What is the purpose of the CFC in a fridge? (Look in a physics book if you need help.)
   (b) When is the CFC in a fridge set free into the air?
   (c) The firm of Bejam offers a CFC recycling scheme for old fridges. How does this help with the ozone problem?

4 The table shows world figures for the production of CFCs.

Year	Mass of CFCs produced (in kilotonne)
1930	0
1940	10
1950	40
1960	140
1965	360
1970	600
1974	800
1975	690
1980	630
1985	690

(a) Plot the mass of CFCs manufactured against the year.
(b) Continue your graph to 1995 to show what you expect to happen to CFC production.
(c) Explain how CFCs could still get into the air for some years even if the production of CFCs were to stop completely.

LEAD IN PETROL: PROFESSORS KNOCK ANTI-KNOCK

A compound of lead called *tetraethyl lead* is added to petrol. It prevents 'knocking'. Knocking is a metallic rattle caused by uneven burning of the petrol vapour.

Lead compounds are sent out of the car exhaust. Recently, scientists have started to worry over the amount of lead that city dwellers breathe in. When people constantly breathe in air containing a lot of lead, lead becomes deposited in their teeth. The Harvard Medical School in the United States have looked into the behaviour and school work of children, and the amount of lead in their teeth. They studied reaction times, the ability to concentrate, the ability to understand words and the results of intelligence tests. Children with a high lead content did less well than those with a low lead content. They also behaved less well.

The UK Government ordered a study on lead pollution. Their panel produced the Lawther Report in 1980. The report blamed paints, foods and cosmetics as the source of lead. The Harvard Report disagreed, blaming lead from car exhausts as the main source of pollution. It suggested that lead in food is derived from the lead in car exhausts. Another report from Professor Bryce-Smith of Reading University and Professor

Stephens of Birmingham University in 1980 also blamed lead in petrol as the main source of lead pollution. They made the startling suggestion that aggressive behaviour may be caused by the effect of lead on the brain. They think it likely that football hooliganism and juvenile delinquency are partly the results of lead poisoning. Their views give us much to think about. Can 'mindless' vandalism really be the result of the effect which lead has on the mind? These responsible research workers have suggested that large numbers of city dwellers are exposed to the possibility of brain damage or personality change through lead poisoning.

One way to avoid pollution in short-distance goods transport

A vigorous campaign over a period of 20 years by the Campaign for Lead-free Air (CLEAR) and other organisations has convinced people that there is danger both from lead compounds in the air and from vegetation that has been contaminated by lead compounds. Many countries have banned tetraethyl lead. The UK has been slow to provide lead-free petrol. From 1990, however, all new vehicles will be designed to run on unleaded petrol. Many petrol stations now sell unleaded petrol, and the number is increasing every week. It is possible to convert many cars to run on unleaded petrol, and many UK drivers are doing this. In March, 1989, the Government encouraged the sale of unleaded petrol by making it 10 p per gallon cheaper than four-star petrol.

There is another advantage of unleaded petrol. Cars can be fitted with catalytic converters (see p. 52-3) to reduce the amounts of other pollutants in exhaust gases. These devices will not work if there is lead in the exhaust gases.

QUESTIONS ON PETROL

1. The table shows petrol prices around the world in November, 1988.

Country	Price in pence per litre		Sales of unleaded petrol as a percentage of total sales
	Unleaded	Four-star	
Denmark	55.4	57.3	32.5
Italy	59.5	58.5	1.3
Japan	63.5	54.5	100
Netherlands	44.9	46.6	26.3
Sweden	38.8	40.7	30.0
Switzerland	32.9	35.6	34.5
UK	36.8	38.0	1.4
USA	17.6	15.1	85.0
West Germany	30.1	30.7	42.0

   (a) List the countries in which unleaded petrol is dearer than leaded petrol.
   (b) Which country leads in sales of unleaded petrol? Why is it so important for this country to avoid pollution?
   (c) Where does the United Kingdom come in the table? Why is the UK less worried about pollution than the country you mentioned in part (b)?

2. In the UK in March 1989, the price of unleaded petrol became 10 p less per gallon than the price of four-star petrol. A motorist paid £20 to have his car converted to run on unleaded petrol. He travels 750 miles a month at 30 miles per gallon. How long will it take him to save the cost of the conversion?

3 Scientists were asked to test the theory that most of the lead in food comes from the soil. They measured the level of lead in cabbages at various distances from a busy road. The inside leaves and outside leaves were measured separately. The table shows their results.

Site	Distance from busy road in metres	Lead levels in cabbage in p.p.m.	
		Outer leaves	Inner leaves
A	1000	0.75	0.15
B	200	0.90	0.25
C	120	3.0	0.20
D	230	0.75	0.20
E	13	2.8	0.30
F	123	1.1	0.20
G	17	7.8	0.70
H	220	5.2	0.30

(a) Show the results either as a graph or as a bar chart.
(b) Do these results support the theory that most of the lead in food comes from the soil? Give reasons for your answer. If you do not agree with the theory, suggest another explanation.
(c) Maximum permitted levels of lead in food are: general food 1.0 p.p.m. (parts per million); baby food 0.2 p.p.m. Comment on how the results in the table compare with these levels.

CARBON MONOXIDE: THE INVISIBLE KILLER

Petrol is a mixture of hydrocarbons. It burns to form carbon dioxide (CO_2) and water. If the supply of air is not plentiful, carbon monoxide (CO) is formed. This is an extremely poisonous gas. One of the dangers of carbon monoxide is that it has no smell to warn you of its presence. If the level of carbon monoxide reaches 0.1 per cent (1000 parts per million) it will kill rapidly. At a tenth of this level (100 p.p.m.) it will give people headaches and stomach pains. The level on London roads has been known to reach 200 p.p.m. for short periods of time. The place where we are in most danger of breathing in carbon monoxide is in traffic jams.

Something can be done about carbon monoxide and other pollutants from car exhausts. Cars in West Germany, Japan, the USA and other countries are fitted with *catalytic converters*. The hot exhaust gases pass through a tube containing a catalyst. The reaction that takes place in the catalytic converter is:

Carbon monoxide + Nitrogen oxide ⟶ Carbon dioxide + Nitrogen
(two pollutants) (two harmless gases)

If the exhaust gases contain lead compounds, the catalyst becomes 'poisoned' and will no longer do its job. Now that unleaded petrol is on sale in the UK, it is possible for British cars to be fitted with catalytic converters. The British motor industry is, however, being very slow to instal the new technology.

Some of the joys of motoring

> Carbon dioxide
> Water vapour
> Carbon monoxide
> Unburnt petrol vapour
> Nitrogen monoxide
> Nitrogen dioxide
> Sulphur dioxide
> Lead vapour

In 1985, the European Community agreed that by 1990 cars would reduce the emission of nitrogen oxide. One way of doing this is by bolting on to car exhausts the catalytic converters described above; another way is by using *lean-burn engines*. The Ford company is spending £550 million in Britain to develop a new lean-burn engine. It uses a higher ratio of air/petrol vapour in the cylinders than present engines do. It burns petrol more efficiently. The temperature in the cylinders is lower, and there is therefore less combination of nitrogen and oxygen to form nitrogen oxide. A lean-burn engine may cut the production of nitrogen oxide by 75 to 90 per cent. The catalytic converters remove carbon monoxide and unburnt hydrocarbons also.

At one time, the pollution in Tokyo was so bad that policemen on traffic duty did only a half-hour spell. When they came off duty, they took a whiff of oxygen from a roadside oxygen dispenser. Thanks to catalytic converters, the Japanese no longer have such a serious problem.

Fuels such as methane (natural gas) and propane burn more easily than petrol. They form the harmless products, carbon dioxide and water. There is some work going on in the motor industry to adapt car engines to run off these fuels.

QUESTION ON ENGINES

Combustion takes place in the cylinders of a petrol engine. The ratio of petrol vapour to air in the cylinders can be altered by 'tuning' the engine. A 'rich' mixture (with a high ratio of petrol/air) gives a smooth engine performance. It also leads to the formation of carbon monoxide and unburnt hydrocarbons. A 'lean' mixture (with a low petrol/air ratio) leads to the formation of nitrogen oxide.

(a) Explain why each of the following is called a pollutant: carbon monoxide, hydrocarbons, nitrogen oxide.
(b) A motorist tunes the engine of his car to increase the ratio of air to fuel in the cylinders. Explain what happens to the amount of each of the pollutants mentioned in part (a) coming from the car exhaust.
(c) How can a motorist get rid of both carbon monoxide and nitrogen oxide before they pollute the environment?

MERCURY: THE MAD HATTER'S COMPLAINT

In some jobs, workers can be exposed to mercury vapour. Mercury is a liquid metal. Some atoms of mercury turn to vapour, and we can breathe in mercury vapour. It affects muscle control. In the manufacture of hats, workers used to use mercury compounds to stiffen the brims. By constantly breathing in small amounts of mercury, they began to suffer from mercury poisoning. They developed 'hatters' shakes'. They lost control of their muscles and their arms and heads shook. At a more advanced stage of the disease, the mind was affected. This is how the expression 'as mad as a hatter' came about.

The Mad Hatter's Tea Party

FLUORIDES

Fluorides are produced by brick-works and aluminium-works. They travel through the air and then fall to earth in the rain. They fall on grass, which is eaten by cows. In *small* quantities fluorides are beneficial. In large quantities, they make the cows' teeth turn black and fall out. They lead to fluorosis, which is a stiffening of the joints, making animals unable to move easily.

QUESTIONS FOR DISCUSSION

QUESTION 1 — What do you think of the idea of banning cars from cities? Who would benefit from this? What arrangements would have to be made for motorists to leave their cars outside the city? What arrangements would have to be made for them to travel into the city and out again? Do you think that our present facilities would be sufficient? Why has this idea never been tried out?

QUESTION 2 — The cost of public transport has risen steeply in recent years. What do you think could be done to encourage people to use public transport more? Remember that a bus company has to make enough money to pay for fuel and repairs and also to buy new buses from time to time and that British Rail wants to make a profit.

QUESTION 3 — Can you think of three advantages of battery-operated cars over petrol-driven cars? Can you think of one disadvantage?

QUESTION 4 — People travel for various reasons. How could people cut down on the amount of petrol they burn (a) for going to work, (b) for going out in the evenings, (c) for going away on trips?

QUESTION 5 — What do you find are the main drawbacks of public transport in your area? What improvements would you make if you were running the bus company?

CIGARETTE SMOKE

Another pollutant in the air is cigarette smoke. It contains many different chemicals. One is carbon monoxide. This is why sitting in a smoke-filled room can give you a headache. Nicotine is another ingredient. It is a stimulant, which enables you to work better, and it is also a tranquilliser. These two effects make nicotine habit-forming. Also present in cigarette smoke are carcinogenic (cancer-forming) hydrocarbons. They are the reason why heavy smokers develop lung cancer. The World Health Organisation estimates that 30 000 people die each year as a result of smoking.

Some people decide that smoking is not worth while. There is the danger of lung cancer. There is the certainty of becoming short of breath and less good at sports. There is the rather nasty 'smoker's cough'. There is the rather unattractive smell of cigarette smoke on the breath. It is very annoying for people who have decided not to smoke to find that they are in a room full of smoke, breathing in other people's nicotine, hydrocarbons and carbon monoxide. Non-smokers are often made to feel very awkward if they ask smokers not to smoke. Should smokers be made to feel selfish if they blow their nicotine and carcinogens over non-smokers? People who inhale smoke from other people's cigarettes are called 'passive smokers'. Passive smokers inhale smoke which has not passed through a filter tip. It is no wonder that passive smokers can suffer from sore eyes, headaches and coughing. There can be more serious results. A passive smoker who lives with a smoker has an increased risk of lung cancer and heart disease. One group of non-smokers who have no say in the matter is the unborn babies. When a pregnant women smokes, some of the chemicals in the cigarette smoke pass through her bloodstream to the unborn baby.

A national child development study in 1978 was made of 800 20-year-olds. Of this group of young people, 95 per cent agreed that smoking can damage your health; 81 per cent agreed that it could cause lung cancer. They know of the dangers, yet 40 per cent of the group smoked; some were heavy smokers (more than 20 a day). Even at the age of 20, they suffered from shortness of breath or wheezing or coughs. Why do 40 per cent of 20-year-olds smoke when they know the dangers?

Some people think that the tax collected by the Government on cigarettes is a big help to the country. You must set against this money the enormous cost of keeping bronchial patients and cancer sufferers in hospital. In 1985–6, smokers paid about £5240 million in taxes on tobacco. The National Health Service spent about £370 million on hospital treatment of people with diseases related to smoking. At work, 50 million working days were lost through illnesses caused by smoking. Of the fires in industry, 20% were caused by careless smoking. The Government spent £4 million on an anti-smoking campaign.

The World Health Organisation has recommended a ban on cigarette advertising. Only 12 countries have followed their lead. Is it advertising that makes young people take up smoking? The advertisements give the impression that it is 'hip' to smoke, that it is 'straight' not to smoke. The advertisers want you to think that it is adult to smoke. Look at the pictures above. Would these people be enjoying themselves less if they were not smoking?

The tobacco manufacturers certainly believe that advertising pays. They spend £80 million a year on advertising.

QUESTIONS AND ACTIVITIES ON SMOKING

1 The table shows the causes of death in 1982 in England and Wales.

Cause of death	Number of deaths
Coronary heart disease	154 600
Lung cancer	38 830
Bronchitis, emphysema and asthma	34 470
Road accidents	5240
Homicide	350

(a) Show these figures in the form of a bar chart.
(b) What was the total number of deaths?

(c) Coronary heart disease, lung cancer, bronchitis, emphysema and asthma are illnesses which are linked with smoking. What was the number of deaths from these causes?

(d) What percentage is the number of deaths from these illnesses of the total number of deaths?

2 **Make a survey of your friends and neighbours**

The bigger the sample of people questioned the better. You may find it more interesting to work in a group of, say, three people.

Question: Do you smoke?	
Answer: Yes	Answer: No
1) Male or female.	1) Male or female.
2) How many cigarettes do you smoke in a day?	2) Have you ever smoked?
3) How long have you been smoking?	3) If you did, why did you stop?
4) Would you like to stop?	4) Do smokers bother you?
5) Have you ever tried to stop?	
6) What made you start smoking?	

(a) Give the numbers of smokers and non-smokers you questioned.

(b) What is the ratio of smokers to non-smokers in your sample?

(c) What fraction of the non-smokers are ex-smokers?

(d) What is the ratio of male smokers to female smokers?

(e) What are the most common reasons for (i) starting to smoke and (ii) stopping smoking?

(f) Draw a bar chart to display the results of your survey. Then draw separate bar charts for male and female smokers. Are there any differences between the patterns for males and females?

3 **A study of lung cancer**

The table gives some information from a study of male doctors in the UK.

Number of cigarettes smoked per day	Number of deaths from lung cancer per 100 000 men per year
0	10
1–14	78
15–24	127
25 or more	251

(a) Describe the apparent link between smoking and cancer.
(b) Joe smokes 10 cigarettes a day. Jim does not smoke. Joe is 8 times more likely to get lung cancer than Jim is. Where does the figure 8 come from?
(c) Ahmed smokes 20 cigarettes a day, and Simon smokes 30. How many times more likely are (i) Ahmed and (ii) Simon to get lung cancer than Jim is?

4 Cigarette advertisements

Cut out cigarette advertisements from magazines and Sunday newspaper colour supplements. Explain how each of the advertisements is designed to be attractive to the public. What do the advertisers seem to promise that smoking will do for the customer?

5 Play your part

Two pupils are needed to play the part of A and B. A is a non-smoker. He or she has taken a seat in a 'No-smoking' carriage in a train. B enters the carriage. A few minutes after the train pulls out of the station, B lights a cigarette.

A: Speak to B to try to persuade him or her to stop smoking.
B: Reply to A.
A: What do you say if B refuses?

Then exchange roles and start again.

6 How to stop

Children aged 11 to 16 spend £90 million a year on cigarettes. If you are one of them, this is how you can stop.

1) Decide on a date, not too far away, when you will stop. Try to get a friend to do the same. Tell all your friends that you are going to stop. Then it will be difficult to wriggle out.

2) Cut down a bit on your smoking before the date arrives. Notice what times of day you normally smoke. Plan to do something at these times to take your mind off smoking.

3) The date arrives. Throw away your cigarettes, lighter, matches, ashtray—everything to do with smoking. Keep telling yourself that you are now a non-smoker. Avoid the occasions on which you used to smoke. Plan a treat for the end of the day, such as an outing or a special meal.

4) The first day is the worst. Before long, your first week will be over. Count up the money you have saved by not smoking. Buy yourself a present. You have earned it!

7 **Talk it out**
This role-play takes two pupils, Chris and Pat. Chris takes the part of a smoker, and Pat takes the part of a non-smoker.
Pat: Give Chris some advice about smoking.
Chris: Say what you feel about giving up. Either defend your habit or put forward a plan for stopping.
Pat: Either try to get Chris to give up or, if Chris has already decided to give up, offer some help with the plan for stopping.

8 **Something for you to do at home**
Advertising of cigarettes is not allowed on television. Tobacco companies try to make up for this by sponsoring sports events which will be televised. Make a copy of this table and fill it in as you watch television over the next month.

Sport	*Name of sponsor*
Football	
Rugby	
County cricket	
Test-match cricket	
Motor-car racing	
Motor-cycle racing	
Snooker	
Others	

(a) Why do some sports need money from sponsors?
(b) In sponsoring sporting events, do tobacco companies promote sport (i) in the short term and (ii) in the long term?
(c) Some people think that sports organisations should not accept money from tobacco companies. Why do they think this? What do you think? Discuss the question with a group of friends to find out what they think.

9 (a) During the six years of the Second World War, 250 000 British people were killed. In the last six years, how many British people died of diseases brought on by smoking? Choose the correct answer.
A. 50 000   B. 100 000   C. 150 000
D. 250 000   E. 500 000
(b) These multiple-choice questions refer to a sample of 1000 young men in England and Wales who smoke 20 cigarettes a day.
(i) How many are likely to die in a road accident?
A. 3   B. 6   C. 9   D. 12   E. 15

(ii) How many are likely to be murdered?
   A. 1   B. 2   C. 3   D. 5   E. 10
(iii) How many are likely to die of diseases brought on by smoking?
   A. 5   B. 50   C. 100   D. 250   E. 500
(Questions 1 and 3 may help you to answer.)

10 How many cigarettes?

The table gives figures about smoking in Britain.

Year	1972	1974	1976	1978	1980	1982	1984
Percentage of men who smoke	52	51	46	45	42	38	36
Percentage of women who smoke	41	41	38	37	37	33	32
Number of cigarettes sold (thousands of millions)	130.5	137.0	130.6	125.0	121.5	102.0	99.0
Number smoked per week per man	120	125	129	127	124	121	115
Number smoked per week per woman	87	94	101	101	102	98	96

(a) When did men non-smokers first outnumber men smokers?
(b) Describe the trend in smoking between 1972 and 1984.
(c) Compare the percentage of men who smoked with the percentage of women who smoked over the years.
(d) Which group showed the biggest change over the years, men or women?
(e) Describe the change in sales of cigarettes over the years.
(f) Give an approximate figure for the percentage change in sales between 1972 and 1984.
(g) Comment on the number of cigarettes per week smoked by women compared with the number smoked by men.
(h) Calculate a value for the number of cigarettes smoked in 1984 as a percentage of those smoked in 1972
   (i) for men and   (ii) for women.

QUESTIONS FOR DISCUSSION

We suggest you organise yourselves into small groups to discuss the following questions.

QUESTION 1

Why do people smoke their first cigarette? Do you think that many people enjoy their first cigarette?

QUESTION 2 Why do friends encourage young people to smoke? Why is it thought to be sociable to accept a cigarette when it is offered?

QUESTION 3 Do you think people take a lot of notice of advertisements? Do you think that the cigarette advertisements really do make people smoke?
If there were no more advertisements for cigarettes, do you think that some people would give up smoking? If advertising stopped, do you think that it would mean fewer young people taking up smoking?

QUESTION 4 Do you think that many smokers would find it hard to give up smoking? What are the disadvantages of a habit which you cannot give up?

QUESTION 5 Do you think that smoking makes a person more interesting or more sociable or more attractive? What do you think of the smell of cigarette smoke on someone's breath? What do you think of 'smoker's cough'?

QUESTION 6 How old do you have to be to buy cigarettes in a shop? Do you think it is wrong for shop-keepers to sell cigarettes to children below this age?

WORDFINDER ON POLLUTION

Can you find the 17 pollutants in the word square below? The answers may read across from left to right or right to left, or diagonally or from top to bottom or bottom to top. There are two words in six of the answers.

```
C K E E P L O O K I N G R S
I A R A F L U O R I D E X U
G T R R E A S R C A S S E L
A M A B R M E O U S N A G P
R Y R D O Y L G L E A D L H
S A N G Y N A R C M O P I U
M G D A R E M A D U S T O R
O A N O U R G O O F O O L D
K I Y B C C O I N L A P E I
E N G E R I F L A O C O S O
O C H R E N E I S R X D E X
D A L I M T G R I T A I I I
X E C O A C F C R E C R D D
P R E P U O S A E P R T O E
```

Copy the word square on to a piece of paper (or photocopy it). One pollutant has been ringed for you, and you can ring the other 16. (Answer on p. 73.)

Do not write on the page.

RADIOACTIVITY

Another type of pollution in the air is *radioactivity*. Some elements have what are termed 'radioactive isotopes'. These are forms of the element which are unstable. The atoms split up to form smaller atoms of different elements. As they split up, the atoms release radiation, and some of the tiny particles of which the atoms are composed escape. The particles and radiation are together called radioactivity. The radiation is very penetrating. It can travel through sheets of metal, through bricks and through concrete.

A certain low level of radioactivity occurs naturally in our surroundings. Our bodies can stand this low level of radiation. But radioactivity is dangerous.

Some people are worried that the level of background radiation may increase to a level which our bodies cannot stand. There are three sources from which people fear that radioactive material may enter the environment. These are:
- (1) nuclear power stations,
- (2) the testing of nuclear weapons, and
- (3) the storage of radioactive waste from nuclear power stations.

Nuclear power stations

We use an enormous amount of energy in our homes, industries and transport. Supplies of coal and petroleum oil are limited. Nuclear energy is our best hope of a source of energy for the future. The level of radioactivity escaping from a nuclear power station is very low. What people are afraid of is an accident.

Nuclear accidents

The world's worst nuclear accident happened at the Russian nuclear power station at Chernobyl in 1986. One of the nuclear reactors exploded and caught fire. The explosion sent streams of radioactive material into the atmosphere. A cloud of radioactive dust drifted across the USSR and Europe for more than a week. The fire burned for four days and it was two weeks before the reactor could be cooled down. The core of a nuclear reactor is intensely hot. This is where nuclear energy is generated from the splitting of uranium atoms. Thousands of gallons of cold water are pumped round it every minute. The cooling system at Chernobyl failed. Although they shut down the reactor, atom-splitting continued and the temperature went up and up. For many days, people were afraid that without cooling water the core would melt and burn through the steel and concrete container. This did not happen because helicopters dropped loads of sand and lead on to the reactor to cool it. Nine days after the explosion, the firefighters fed cold nitrogen into the reactor. The idea was to cool the reactor and to keep out oxygen. Fortunately, the idea worked, but it was 12 days after the accident when they put out the fire.

What was the damage? Thirty-one people died, 200 people were sent to hospital with severe radiation sickness, 135 000 people were evacuated from 180 towns and villages in the area. People far from the reactor may have received enough radiation to make them develop cancer or leukaemia. Leukaemia is a disease in which the body stops making red blood cells. It is estimated that 5000 people will die prematurely from the doses of radiation they received. Huge clouds of radioactive dust spread over the surrounding countryside, the Ukraine, where much of the grain that the USSR produces is grown. The contamination will last for many years. Radioactive dust settled on countries throughout Europe. Sweden reckoned that £100 million worth of crops had been contaminated. When the cloud reached the UK, radioactive dust settled on pasture land, and £10 million worth of sheep were contaminated by eating grass.

How did it happen? Incredibly, the accident happened during the course of a safety test. The team of technicians had disconnected automatic safety systems, the systems that shut down the reactor if it becomes dangerously hot. This action was against the rules for operating the reactor. The cooling water overheated and turned into steam. Chemical reactions between steam and graphite and between steam and metals produced hydrogen. It was this hydrogen that caused the explosion and the fire. After the chemical explosion, the reactor got out of control. There was a danger of a nuclear explosion. Soviet experts say that the reactor came close to exploding like a nuclear bomb.

Could it happen here? The Russian investigation found that the cause of the accident was human error. The team responsible for the reactor had made six serious mistakes. They had failed to follow safety instructions. The director of the plant, the chief engineer and four other people were sent to prison. Experts in other countries say that the Russian reactor is of a poor design. It runs at a high temperature, and it is water-cooled. There is always a danger of a leak in the cooling pipes. If this happens, steam comes into contact with red-hot graphite, and a chemical reaction produces hydrogen. When hydrogen meets air, an explosion is bound to follow. British reactors are gas-cooled. The gas is carbon dioxide, which is much less chemically reactive than steam.

It is not only in the USSR that there have been accidents. There was an accident in the British nuclear power station at Sellafield in 1953. Nuclear power stations have as many as four back-up cooling systems, for use if the first system fails. In spite of such precautions, there was an emergency at Three Mile Island in the United States in 1980. The temperature of the reactor rose after the cooling system was accidentally turned off, and some radioactive material was released.

Three Mile Island nuclear power station

Testing of nuclear weapons

The major world powers have built up stocks of nuclear weapons. They want to test these weapons. If there is a trial detonation of an atomic bomb, radioactive material flies up into the atmosphere. It may be blown by the wind far away from the place where the bomb was exploded before it falls to earth in the rain. Then it seeps into the soil to be absorbed by grass. When cows eat the grass, some radioactive material passes into their bodies. When these cows give milk, some radioactive material passes out in the milk. When we drink the milk, we are drinking some radioactivity with it.

Strontium is an element which resembles calcium. A radioactive form of strontium called strontium-90 is formed in nuclear explosions. It is very dangerous as it passes into cows' milk, just as calcium does, and, if we drink it, it is built into our bones and teeth, just as calcium is. The radioactivity of strontium-90 lasts for a very long time. Once you have some strontium-90 in your bones, it will go on irradiating you for the rest of your life.

As a result of this danger, all the 'nuclear' countries in the world have united in banning nuclear testing above ground. All tests are now carried out deep underground.

Storage of radioactive waste

In nuclear power stations, radioactive waste is produced. Some radioactive waste is sealed in steel containers and dumped far out at sea. This practice is not as safe as it was thought to be, as some of the canisters are showing signs of rusting. Liquids of high activity are stored in tanks made of stainless steel and surrounded by concrete.

Deep burial now seems to be the best way of storing radioactive waste. In West Germany and the United States, canisters of radioactive waste are stored deep underground in disused salt mines. The danger of pollution of the air or water supply is less than in other methods of storage. The radioactive material must be stored until it is no longer radioactive. This is a very long time. Strontium-90 has a *half-life* of 29 years. This means that after 29 years, half of the radioactivity will be left. After 58 years, a quarter will be left. After 116 years, $\frac{1}{16}$th of the radioactivity will be left. Before strontium-90 produced this year is safe to throw away, it will have to be kept for 500 years. Generation after generation will have to keep a check on it, to make sure that the steel tank is still safe and that there is no leakage. Plutonium-239 has a half-life of 24 000 years. How long will plutonium-239 need to be stored before it can be thrown away? The type of nuclear reactor called a *breeder reactor* produces plutonium-239.

SOME POLLUTION ACTIVITIES

ACTIVITY 1

How pure is the air you breathe? The lichens will tell you

Lichens are plants which grow on trees, walls and stones. They grow all the year round. Because they are sensitive to sulphur dioxide, no lichens will grow in the most polluted air. Some lichens will grow in inner city areas, especially on basic materials such as concrete and limestone, which neutralise the sulphur dioxide in the air. Other lichens will grow only in the purest air.

By making a lichen search and noting where different types of lichen grow, you can map the purity of the air in your neighbourhood. The illustrations below show five types of lichen. If you are interested in this out-of-school activity, you can obtain more information from a book such as *The Observer Book of Lichens*.

Pleurococcus

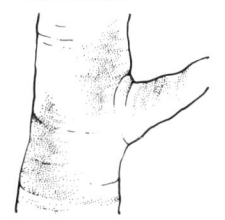

Lecanora

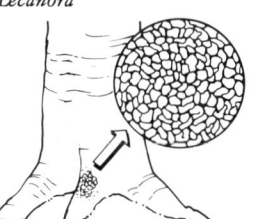

Xanthoria

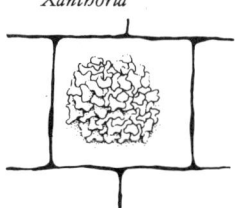

The most polluted air
No lichens.
Bright green powdery algae in trees.

A high degree of pollution
The only lichens are scaly lichens, e.g. *Lecanora* (green on trees, white on concrete) and *Xanthoria* (orange, found on stone).

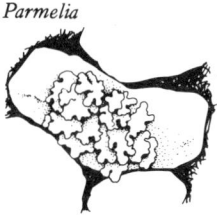

Parmelia

Evernia

Usnea

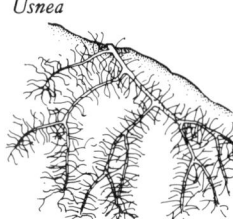

Lichens

Slightly polluted air
In addition to the scaly lichens, leafy lichens, such as *Parmelia*, are found. If you find them on trees, you know the air is purer than if they grow only on basic stones, such as concrete and limestone.

Unpolluted air
In addition to the other lichens, shrubby lichens, such as *Evernia* and *Usnea* (a tangle of delicate green threads) are found.

ACTIVITY 2

Collecting dust

The amount of dust falling out of the air can be measured. To do this, you need some sticky cards which can be bought from laboratory suppliers. If you remove the protective backing paper, the cards will collect dust, soot and pollen grains. The idea is to leave the cards in different positions in the area you are investigating. After a few days, you can collect them and examine them under a microscope.

ACTIVITY 3 — Looking at smoke

Laboratory suppliers sell Ringelmann smoke charts. You hold up the chart and compare it with the smoke coming from a chimney. If the smoke is a denser grey than grade 2 on the chart, and continues to be so for some time, then the house or factory is breaking the Clean Air Act.

To complete Activities 4, 5 and 6, you will have to ask your teacher for detailed instructions.

ACTIVITY 4 — What gases are put into the air when coal burns?

ACTIVITY 5 — What gases are put into the air when petroleum products burn?

ACTIVITY 6 — Making and testing sulphur dioxide

ACTIVITY 7 — Does sulphur dioxide affect plants?

The diagram below shows how you can find out what sulphur dioxide does to plants. Sodium metabisulphite is a compound which reacts slowly with water to form sulphur dioxide. (It is the compound used in sterilising equipment for home beer-making.) A little tray made out of aluminium foil holds a few crystals of sodium metabisulphite and a little water. A clump of cress plants and the tray are put into a crystallising dish and enclosed in a polythene bag. A control experiment is set up without sodium metabisulphite. After 2 days, you will begin to see a difference between the two clumps of plants.

Cress and sulphur dioxide

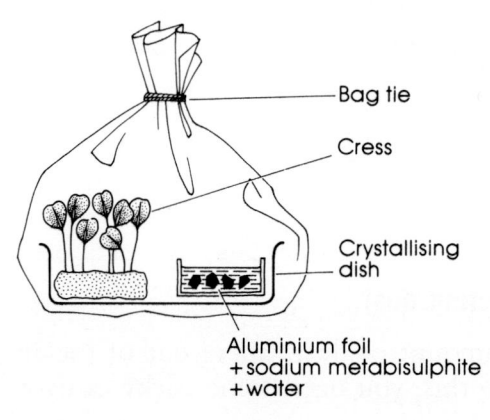

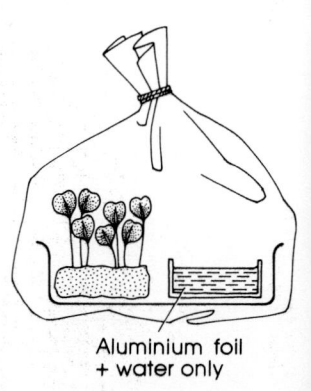

Bag tie
Cress
Crystallising dish
Aluminium foil + sodium metabisulphite + water

Aluminium foil + water only

ACTIVITY 8

What do cigarettes deposit in your lungs?

The diagram below shows a cigarette-smoking apparatus. If you do this experiment, you will find out what one cigarette deposits in your lungs. Try to imagine this multiplied by 20 for each day. This is what smokers are doing to their lungs.

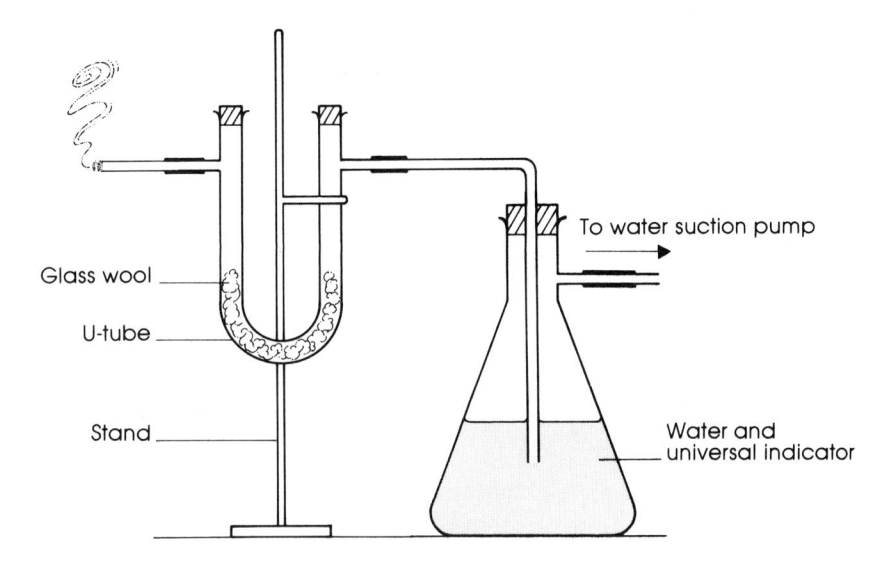

Smoking a cigarette

QUESTIONS ON POLLUTION

1. The diagram shows hot exhaust gases from a car engine entering a catalytic converter.

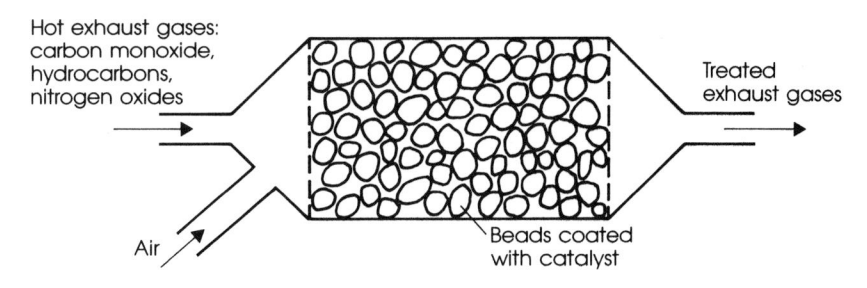

    (a) What is a *catalyst*?
    (b) What is each of the gases shown in the diagram changed into by the converter?

2. (a) Draw a diagram to show how rain becomes acidic.
    (b) Suggest one reason why sulphur dioxide from other parts of Europe ends up in Norway and Sweden.
    (c) Name two acids which are present in acid rain and snow.
    (d) Suggest why, in Sweden, (i) rain is more acidic during winter and (ii) lakes are more acidic in the springtime.

CROSSWORD ON AIR POLLUTION

First, trace this grid on to a piece of paper (or photocopy this page). Then fill in the answers. Do not write on this page.

Across

6 _____ smog is a kind of pollution formed in sunlight (13)
8 A temperature _____ can occur in a hot, low-lying area (9)
9 It consists of water droplets in the air (3)
10 Hydrocarbons can replace CFCs in aerosol _____ (4)
12, 15 down   Large quantities of fluorides can give cows _____ _____ (5, 5)
15 An irritant may bring this to your eye (4)
16, 21 down   It was passed by Parliament in 1956 (5, 3, 3)
17 Pollution can get into food we _____ (3)
19 Don't say _____ if offered a cigarette! (3)
20 A lichen (5)
22 It blamed lead from car exhausts as the main source of pollution (7, 6)

Down

1 If this is tall, the factory smoke won't bother you (7)
2 Chemicals that may pollute by corroding (5)
3 Colour of a 'pea-souper' (6)
4 It can pollute our beaches (3)
5 The _____ kind of pollution is long-lasting (11)
7 A pollutant that affects muscle control (7)
11 A _____ power station produces 5 down waste (7)
13 Cigarettes are no good for your _____ (5)
14 One of the places where radio-active material is dumped (3)
15 See 12 across
18 A pollutant from cigarettes (3)
20 _____ cars less to reduce pollution (3)
21 See 16 across

SUMMARY OF POLLUTION

Pollutant	Main Source	Effects of the pollutant
Smoke	Factories and homes	Makes buildings and clothes dirty. Cuts down sunlight. Affects plant growth. Affects breathing. Causes chest and bronchial complaints.
Grit and dust	Factories	Make buildings and clothes dirty. Can get into machinery and cause difficulties.
Sulphur dioxide	Factories and cars	A choking gas. It dissolves in water to form sulphurous acid. Oxygen changes this to sulphuric acid, a strong acid. This attacks plants, buildings and metals.
Lead	Cars	Poisonous. Affects the brain. Large doses cause blindness and brain damage. It is thought that smaller doses may result in poor concentration and anti-social behaviour.
Carbon monoxide	Cars	A poisonous gas. Its lack of smell makes it dangerous. Small doses cause headaches and drowsiness. Large doses kill.
Nitrogen oxides	Cars	In sunlight lead to the formation of photochemical smog.
Hydrocarbons	Cars	
Mercury	Industries	Poisonous. Affects muscle control. Large doses kill.
Fluoride	Brick-works, aluminium-works	Falls on grass. Leads to fluorosis in cattle (a disease of the joints).

What can be done?

Factories: Make chimneys tall. Use smokeless fuels. Study ways of making fuel burn completely to harmless products.

Homes: Use smokeless fuels.

Cars: Stop adding lead to petrol. Refine sulphur out of petrol. Change to fuels which burn more completely than petrol. Fit catalytic converters to cars. Use battery-operated cars.

Public Transport: An improvement in public transport would cut down on the use of cars.

MORE QUESTIONS ON POLLUTION

Supply the missing words for questions 1–4. Do not write on this page.

1. Fog is formed when air containing a lot of water vapour is suddenly _____. It consists of _____ of water. Fog lasts longest on days when there is little _____. Smoke contains particles of _____. These particles are formed during the _____ of fuels. A mixture of smoke and fog is called _____.

2. City air is hot. Hot air _____ and takes pollution with it. Cold air moves _____ to take its place. In a very hot climate, the Sun warms the air above the city. A temperature _____ may occur. The air above the city becomes even _____ than the city air. The city air is _____ and cannot _____. The intense sunlight causes the formation of _____ smog.

3. The dangerous gas present in smog is _____. It is formed by burning fuels which contain _____. Breathing in a lot of this gas can cause illness such as _____. The reason why this gas irritates the lungs and throat is that it dissolves in water to form _____ acid. In air, this acid forms the stronger acid, _____ acid.

4. Factories burn _____ and _____. To avoid expelling their waste gases at street level, they have _____ _____. In a smokeless zone, factories and homes burn fuel which contains less _____ than average. They produce less _____ than average.

5. Write a short story about a foggy day. Your story should contain three incidents in which people get into difficulties or have accidents due to the fog.

6. What events led Parliament to pass the Clean Air Act in 1956?

7. State three ways in which the gas sulphur dioxide costs us money.

8. Petrol-driven vehicles produce much of the pollution in the air. What harmful substances are given out by these vehicles? How could these pollutants be reduced?

9. What steps have been taken in London to minimise the chances of smog returning?

10. What is the difference between smog and photochemical smog?

11. Why is photochemical smog limited to places like Los Angeles and Tokyo?

12 Much of the sulphur dioxide in the air is from power stations and factories. Suggest two ways in which the output of sulphur dioxide could be reduced.

13 It is believed that death from bronchitis is often caused by high levels of sulphur dioxide. Where in the United Kingdom are people most likely to die from bronchitis? Where are the safest areas to live to escape the disease?

14 What purpose does the ozone layer in the upper atmosphere serve? What is likely to use up some of the ozone layer?

15 What are the advantages of (a) petrol-driven vehicles and (b) battery-powered vehicles?

16 Supply words to fill in the blanks. Do not write on this page.
Radioactive elements give off harmful ____. The time needed for radioactivity to fall to half its original level is called the ____ of the radioactive element. Strontium-90 is a radioactive element which resembles ____. Because of this resemblance, strontium-90 is laid down in ____ and ____. Radioactive material gets into the air from ____ power stations and from the testing of ____ weapons.

17 Why is radioactive waste stored instead of being thrown out straight away? How are radioactive solids stored? How are radioactive liquids stored?

ANSWER TO WORDFINDER ON P. 62

Cigar smoke, smog, fluoride, lead, dust, dirt, mercury, fog, diesel oil, petrol fumes, carbon monoxide, coal fire, pea-souper, grit, sulphur dioxide, oil, CFC.

ANSWERS TO NUMERICAL QUESTIONS

Chapter 1

p. 14   7   (b) (i) 800 kilotonne   (ii) 17 000 kilotonne
            (c) 51

Chapter 2

p. 51   2   8 months
p. 57   1   (b) 233 490   (c) 227 900   (d) 98%
p. 58   3   (c) (i) 13   (ii) 25
p. 60   9   (a) E.   (b) (i) B.   (ii) A.   (iii) D.
p. 61   10 (h) (i) 96%   (ii) 110%

73

INDEX

Acid rain 37
Acropolis 34
Aerosols 44
Amazon rain forest 19
Ammonia 11
Antarctic 45
Arctic 46

Bosch process 11
Brazil 19

Carbon cycle 16
Carbon dioxide 16
Carbon monoxide 52
Catalytic converters 52
Central Electricity Generating Board, CEGB 41
Chernobyl 63-5
Chlorofluorocarbons, CFCs 17, 19, 45, 47
Cigarette smoke 55, 57, 59, 69
Cloud formation 29
Coal gasification 40
Concorde 45, 46
Crosswords 7, 15, 25, 70

Debt swap 20
Deforestation 20
Divers' air supply 3
Divers' 'bends' 26
Drax Power Station 41
Dust collection 67

Fertiliser route 10
Fertilisers 8
Fish deaths 38
Flue gas desulphurisation, FGD 41
Fluorides 55
Forestry Commission 39
Fossil fuels 18

Gases in air 1
Greenhouse effect 17
Guano 10

Haber process 11

Lakes 38
Lead 49
Lean-burn engines 53
Lichens 67
Lung power 28

Mercury 54
Montreal Protocol 47

Neon lights 26
Nitric acid 11, 37
Nitrogen cycle 9
Nitrogen oxides 30, 33, 37
Noble gases 26
Nuclear power 63
Nuclear waste 66
Nuclear weapons 65

Ostwald process 11
Oxygen 2-5
Ozone layer 44-9

Photochemical smog 33
Photosynthesis 22
Pollutants 30-72
Pulverised fluidised bed combustion, PFBC 41

Radioactive waste 66
Radioactivity 63
Renewable energy sources 41
Respiration 22
Ringelmann chart 68

Smog 31, 33
Smokeless fuels 33
Smokeless zones 32
Space shuttle 5
Sulphur dioxide 31, 32, 33, 34, 37, 68
Sulphuric acid 32, 36, 37

Temperature inversion 34

Unleaded petrol 51
USSR 46, 63-5

Wordfinder 62